"The relationship between identity and the sacraments is a fascinating and timely subject, and Kevin Emmert is a judicious and thoughtful guide. Even people who differ slightly in their understanding of baptism and Communion, as I do, will benefit from reading this book, thinking through the issues, and reflecting on how it can shape disciples today."

Andrew Wilson, Teaching Pastor, King's Church London

"One major problem in the Christian ecclesiastical imagination is that somehow we 'do' church. That is both incorrect and harmful, but it plays well in a world where individuals consider their lives to be those of free self-construction and thus worship to be a matter of spontaneity and human creativity. Of the many ways of exposing and correcting this faulty vision, Kevin Emmert offers one of the most powerful: reflection on the sacraments not as things we 'do' but as gifts from God by which he binds us to himself. Evangelical neglect of the sacraments has taken a heavy toll on church life and has fueled our inability to resist the siren call of expressivism. This book teaches pastors and laypeople that a large part of the answer to this complicated problem lies in the simplicity of sacramental practice."

Carl R. Trueman, Professor of Biblical and Religious Studies, Grove City College; author, *The Rise and Triumph of the Modern Self*

"In our day, questions around personal identity are swirling and ever present. And Christians are not immune from the upheaval and confusion. Kevin Emmert's book looks for help in what for many Christians might seem an unlikely place: the sacraments. *The Water and the Blood*, however, is not a partisan plea for a particular view of baptism and Communion. Instead, Emmert presents a compelling and winsome case to all Christians for the value of the rites and symbols of the historic church. Here we learn that the sacraments confirm our identity as those united to Christ and inspire us to live accordingly. Emmert demonstrates how the sacraments bring purpose, meaning, and joy to our lives and invite us to live a story worth telling."

Brian S. Rosner, Principal, Ridley College, Melbourne, Australia

"Amid today's desperate and hollow quest for 'identity,' Kevin Emmert reminds us that to be a Christian means not only to identify *with* Christ but also to be *in* Christ. And the gateways of grace through which God draws us into Christ and forms us in his image are the very sacraments of baptism and Communion given us by Christ in Scripture."

Joel Scandrett, Associate Professor of Historical Theology, Trinity School for Ministry; executive editor, *To Be a Christian: An Anglican Catechism*

"In an age when many struggle with questions of identity, Kevin Emmert helpfully points to the sacraments as identity-forming activities that can teach us in tangible ways what it means to be persons united to Christ. *The Water and the Blood* offers a practical guide to how baptism and Communion can shape our identity and daily lives as believers joined to Christ. This work, steeped in Scripture and biblical insights from historical Protestant confessions and Christian thinkers, inspires all types of Protestants to reconsider baptism and Communion as critical identity-shaping rites."

Karin Spiecker Stetina, Associate Professor of Biblical and Theological Studies, Talbot School of Theology, Biola University

"Saturated in Scripture and the best of the Christian tradition, this book has a word for us that is too good and beautiful to ignore. Far from baptism and the Lord's Supper being empty signs of an absent Christ, they are safe harbor, true sustenance, and, yes, identity markers. For at font and table, in the life-giving presence of our Lord, we learn *whose* we are and thus *who* we are. Read this book! It is full of wisdom and gospel truth—a balm and bulwark against the modern malaise surrounding authentic personhood."

John C. Clark, Professor of Theology, Moody Bible Institute; coauthor, *The Incarnation of God* and *A Call to Christian Formation*

"Identity seems to be the preoccupation of our time. Unfortunately, we tend to look in all the wrong places to find it—some inward, others to the fickle affirmation of others. This book lights the path to a better way. Kevin Emmert shows how only Christ provides a solid foundation for our identity and how we encounter him afresh through the sacraments. With deep yet accessible theology, Emmert demonstrates how the sacraments help form our identity in Christ in a dynamic and tangible way. *The Water and the Blood* is a profound and beautiful book that will resonate with believers from a variety of traditions."

Drew Dyck, author, *Yawning at Tigers* and *Your Future Self Will Thank You*

"Our culture has sent us and the people we love on a wild goose chase in search of our true selves. Rather than deliver on its promises of authenticity, this chase has left us anxious, divided, and confused. Kevin Emmert's *The Water and the Blood* points us in a better way, showing how the heavenly gifts of baptism and the Eucharist have bolstered the people of God in their secure and tangible identity in Christ in every era. Richly researched and pastorally attuned, this volume will help every pastor and Christian exchange the wild goose chase for the still waters and green pastures of our good shepherd."

Aaron Damiani, Rector, Immanuel Anglican Church, Chicago; author, *Earth Filled with Heaven: Finding Life in Liturgy, Sacraments, and Other Ancient Practices of the Church*

The Water and the Blood

The Water and the Blood

How the Sacraments Shape Christian Identity

Kevin P. Emmert

CROSSWAY®

WHEATON, ILLINOIS

The Water and the Blood: How the Sacraments Shape Christian Identity
© 2023 by Kevin P. Emmert
Published by Crossway
    1300 Crescent Street
    Wheaton, Illinois 60187

Cover painting and design: Micah Lanier

First printing 2023

Printed in the United States of America

Trade paperback ISBN: 978-1-4335-8499-2
ePub ISBN: 978-1-4335-8502-9
PDF ISBN: 978-1-4335-8500-5

Library of Congress Cataloging-in-Publication Data

Names: Emmert, Kevin P., 1986– author.
Title: The water and the blood : how the sacraments shape Christian identity / Kevin P. Emmert.
Description: Wheaton, Illinois : Crossway, 2023. | Includes bibliographical references and index.
Identifiers: LCCN 2022060725 (print) | LCCN 2022060726 (ebook) | ISBN 9781433584992 (trade paperback) | ISBN 9781433585005 (pdf) | ISBN 9781433585029 (epub)
Subjects: LCSH: Baptism. | Lord's Supper. | Sacraments.
Classification: LCC BV803 .E66 2023 (print) | LCC BV803 (ebook) | DDC 234/.161—dc23/eng/20230523
LC record available at https://lccn.loc.gov/2022060725
LC ebook record available at https://lccn.loc.gov/2022060726

Crossway is a publishing ministry of Good News Publishers.

BP		32	31	30	29	28	27	26	25	24	23
15	14	13	12	11	10	9	8	7	6	5	4	3	2	1

For Ashley, Jack, Charlie, and Noah

Contents

Preface

COUNTLESS PEOPLE TODAY STRUGGLE to understand themselves, and they are looking in all sorts of directions to find who they are. Christians, however, do not need to look far to discover their identity. Answers to their questions regarding personal meaning, significance, and purpose lie right before their eyes in the context of God's people gathered for worship—specifically in the rites and symbols of the historic church.

This book, therefore, is about the sacraments. But it is not a typical book about the sacraments. It is not limited to discussing the nature and purpose of baptism and Communion, though it certainly does explore those features in detail. Nor is it polemical, arguing for, say, a specific mode of baptism, whether the infants of Christian parents can or should be baptized, or whether (and, if so, in what manner) Christ is present in the bread and the cup. This is primarily a book on what the sacraments reveal to us about being persons in Christ, about what it means to have our identity and purpose as Christians constituted in him. It is about what it means to be baptized persons, persons immersed into Christ and into the communion of saints. Therefore, it is also a book on the doctrine of union with Christ and what that doctrine means for the self. This study is my attempt as a scholar, active church member, husband, and father to attain a firmer grasp of what it means to be joined to Christ and his body and what that union means for personal identity. The sacraments have far more to teach us about our identity as in-Christ persons than we realize. Christ and his benefits are presented to us in baptism and Communion, and as we embrace him more fully, we come to understand more profoundly who we are in him.

While I am writing from my own ecclesial context as an Anglican of Reformed convictions, I attempt to appeal to Protestants of various stripes. I have in mind especially those who tend to embrace a "low ecclesiology." This demographic typically possesses a minimalistic understanding of the sacraments (and often prefers the term *ordinances*) and thus ascribes them little value in corporate worship. My goal is to set forth what many Protestants have historically agreed on regarding the sacraments while at the same time challenging them to think more deeply on what the sacraments teach us about being persons in Christ. I want readers to know that the gifts of God for the people of God—baptism and Communion—reveal to us who we are in Christ. These visible words of the gospel have power to shape our understanding of Christ and of ourselves, as well as to subvert worldly notions of the self and personal identity. Many people today are seeking to discover themselves through self-referential means, and the result is confusion. For Christians, identity is not constructed but revealed. It is not self-generated but received. Identity is given in Christ and ratified in the gospel sacraments he has ordained.

Just as our identity as Christians is not self-constructed, neither is this book the product of self-isolated exercise. Most of this book was written not in my office or in a study but at my family's dining table. It was informed by family life and crafted at the center of family life, at the very spot where my family and I enjoy food, Scripture, prayer, and singing—together and with our guests. And so I dedicate this book to my precious family. Ashley, my dear wife and closest companion: I cannot find the words to express just how incredible your love and support is, which you show me day after day, year after year. In so many ways—more than you know—you show me what it looks like to live in Christ and like Christ. Your self-sacrificial love and service are both beautiful and humbling. Thank you for your constant encouragement as I wrote this book and for all the helpful suggestions you provided. You are an incredible editor and—far more importantly—a godly woman. You make my work and life unspeakably better than what it would be without you. My sons, Jack, Charlie, and Noah: Thank you for your joy and energy, which bring me so much happiness. And thank you for your patience as I wrote this book. I am proud to be your father. May the three of you lay hold of your baptismal identity and enjoy a long life of sweet communion with our Lord.

I am also grateful for my friends Meghan Robins, Will Chester, and John Clark. Each of you read various portions of an ever-evolving manuscript and provided keen insight for improvements. John, you in particular read my drafts carefully and offered numerous helpful suggestions for both content and phrasing. This book is better because of your thoughtful contribution, wordsmithery, and godly encouragement.

Several of my Crossway colleagues were also hugely instrumental in the development of this book. Samuel James, you helped me tremendously at the early stages as I was still outlining the book, and you provided incredibly valuable feedback on every chapter. David Barshinger, you made numerous edits and suggestions that greatly improved my work. Thank you for your keen editorial eye and theological expertise. I am honored to work with both of you.

I must also recognize my church family. I could not have written this book without participating in the joyful liturgical work performed week in and week out by the congregation. My own church and ecclesial tradition have given me greater clarity of what it means to enact our in-Christ identity. As we gather around the font and approach the table, in living union with the one holy catholic and apostolic church, I learn more of what it means to be immersed into Christ and to commune with him.

And with that, I gladly acknowledge that this book seeks to be confessional-theological, done in the context of the church and for the church. It aims to confess what Holy Scripture teaches about who we are in Christ and to offer a theological account that is connected to faithful, historic Christian dogma. When we come to understand more who Christ is and what he has done and what it means to be in him, we come to understand more deeply and joyfully who we are.

Abbreviations

ANF	*Ante-Nicene Fathers*. Edited by Alexander Roberts, James Donaldson, and A. Cleveland Cox. 10 vols. 1885–1887. Reprint, Peabody, MA: Hendrickson, 1995.
BCP	Anglican Church in North America. *The Book of Common Prayer*. Huntington Beach, CA: Anglican Liturgy Press, 2019.
BDAG	Danker, Frederick W., Walter Bauer, William F. Arndt, and F. Wilbur Gingrich. *Greek-English Lexicon of the New Testament and Other Early Christian Literature*. 3rd ed. Chicago: University of Chicago Press, 2000.
BNTC	Black's New Testament Commentaries
CCC	*Creeds, Confessions, and Catechisms: A Reader's Edition*. Edited by Chad Van Dixhoorn. Wheaton, IL: Crossway, 2022.
CNTC	Calvin's New Testament Commentaries
Inst.	Calvin, John. *Institutes of the Christian Religion*. Edited by John T. McNeill. Translated by Ford Lewis Battles. Philadelphia: Westminster John Knox, 1960.

NIGTC	New International Greek Testament Commentary
NPNF[1]	*Nicene and Post-Nicene Fathers.* Series 1. Edited by Philip Schaff. 14 vols. Buffalo, NY: Christian Literature, 1886–1890.
NSBT	New Studies in Biblical Theology
PG	Patrologia Graeca. Edited by J.-P. Migne. 162 vols. Paris, 1857–1886.
SSBT	Short Studies in Biblical Theology
WCF	Westminster Confession of Faith
WLC	Westminster Larger Catechism
WSC	Westminster Shorter Catechism
WTJ	*Westminster Theological Journal*

Introduction

The Problem of the Christian Self

IN AN AGE WHEN COUNTLESS PEOPLE are struggling to understand their identity, Christians frequently tell one another, "Your
identity is in Christ." This statement is often issued in attempts
to swiftly tranquilize anxiety when someone expresses uncertainty
over place and purpose in life: Who am I? Do I belong? How do
I find security? What is my purpose? Yet in many such cases, the
adage does little to assuage unwelcome feelings of bewilderment.
People often tout it without much elaboration, and thus it feels like
a trope. Truthfully, the statement is pregnant with rich theology
and deserves greater reflection—especially in an age when many
Christians are operating with a confused or undeveloped sense of
self. In our day, too many Christians do not rightly understand
the Christian self and what bearing their identity in Christ has on
their identity as particular persons.

At the core of the statement that the Christian's identity is in
Christ is the biblical truth that our very existence *as Christians* is
constituted in and determined by the living, active, and present
Christ. The Christian self is a self *in Christ*. Put differently, being

in Christ is our primary identity as Christians. This is true because Jesus Christ, the Son of God incarnate, is the God-man. As both God and man, he is not only the one true mediator between God and humanity but also the true revelation of both God and humanity. He alone truly reveals both who God is and who we are.

Trying to understand this unfathomable truth helps us navigate the tides of modern secular culture, which is obsessed with self-understanding and self-actualization. One of the greatest absurdities today is that many of us Christians have followed the world's advice on how to find a place and purpose in life. Our world tells us to look at ourselves in order to discover ourselves.[1] With mantras like "Be true to yourself" and "You do you," we are conditioned to believe that we are individuals who determine our own identities and can express them however we want.[2] But the more we look at ourselves, the more confused we become over who we are. Indeed, the path to self-discovery and self-actualization leads only to despair. While the notion that identity is self-generated is a relatively recent development, the truth is that looking inward, in a manner that is self-focused, is not a uniquely modern disposition. It is the inclination of sinful humans, the proclivity we all have inherited from our primal parents. When Adam and Eve erred, they imme-

---

1 A 2015 study found that 91 percent of US adults agreed that the best way to find oneself is by looking within oneself. See David Kinnaman and Gabe Lyons, *Good Faith: Being a Christian When Society Thinks You're Irrelevant and Extreme* (Grand Rapids, MI: Baker, 2016), 58.

2 Many have called this phenomenon "expressive individualism" and the age of "authenticity." On the development of such a phenomenon and critical analysis of it, see, e.g., Charles Taylor, *A Secular Age* (Cambridge, MA: Belknap Press of Harvard University Press, 2007); Carl R. Trueman, *The Rise and Triumph of the Modern Self: Cultural Amnesia, Expressive Individualism, and the Road to the Sexual Revolution* (Wheaton, IL: Crossway, 2020). My aim in this book is not to show how such ideas now rampant in our modern world have developed but to offer a theological framework that can help Christians work through their feelings of anxiety and uncertainty with regard to who they are.

diately gazed at themselves and were engulfed in fear and shame. What is significant about this act of looking at ourselves is that it coincides with turning away from God. This is precisely the danger of looking at ourselves to understand who we are, for when we do, we turn away from the power that constitutes our very being. So in our constant search to find ourselves by looking at ourselves, we are actually losing ourselves.[3]

If we as Christians want to understand who we are—to know what significance, place, and purpose we have—we must fix our gaze on Jesus Christ because he is the one who has constituted our very existence. We can rightly understand *who we are* only in relation to *who he is*. Personal identity is therefore not something we must discover on our own through our own narratives and pursuits but is something already granted to us in the Lord Jesus Christ. Simply put, our identity is not a construct to self-fabricate but a gift to receive.

How to Understand Ourselves

One of the most powerful tools for helping us understand ourselves in relation to Christ is the sacraments. As historic rites of the church, baptism and Communion are characteristic of the church—her belief, identity, life, and practices. They reveal, in palpable form, who the church is and what she is about, and they do the same for her particular members. To be sure, the sacraments testify chiefly to who Christ is and to what God has done for us in Christ. Yet these divine gifts—alongside and never in competition with the gift of Scripture—also proclaim to us what it means to be persons in Christ. As visible and tangible confirmations of God's

---

3 I am indebted to John C. Clark for this expression.

work in Christ, the sacraments therefore give flesh and bones to the statement that the Christian's identity is in Christ and thus provide an effective antidote to the problems so many Christians today face in understanding their identity and purpose. Stated differently, baptism and Communion are identity-forming rituals that teach us in touchable and accessible ways what it means to be persons in Christ.

Further, because the sacraments are outward and visible signs of inward and spiritual graces—to use the language of Augustine,[4] which has been embraced by countless Christians throughout history—they offer aesthetic appeal in a time when many Christians are being allured and catechized by ungodly narratives and practices. Carl Trueman has urged the church to "reflect long and hard on *the connection between aesthetics and her core beliefs and practices.*"[5] He rightly observes that personal narratives have become the highest authority in our modern world, which means that personal narratives are the arbiter for ethics and morality. To this we can add images, which, as Mario Vargas Llosa explains, "have primacy over ideas. For that reason, cinema, television and now the Internet have left books to one side."[6] This is evident, Trueman argues, in that people's opinions on gay marriage and complex political issues—to name just a few examples—are shaped nowadays primarily by "aesthetics through images created by camera angles and plotlines in movies, sitcoms, and soap operas."[7] Or as Jonathan Gottschall remarks, "People can be made to think differently about sex, race,

---

4 See Augustine, *On the Catechizing of the Uninstructed*, trans. S. D. F. Salmond, in *NPNF*[1] 3:312 (26.50).

5 Trueman, *Rise and Triumph*, 402; emphasis original.

6 Mario Vargas Llosa, *Notes on the Death of Culture: Essays on Spectacle and Society*, trans. John King (New York: Picador, 2012), 37, quoted in Trueman, *Rise and Triumph*, 403.

7 Trueman, *Rise and Triumph*, 403.

class, gender, violence, ethics, and just about anything else based on a single short story or television show."[8] The stories and images presented to us on a daily basis are shaping not just our views on morality but also our sense of self, for, as Charles Taylor has shown, morality is inextricably linked to identity.[9]

If our morality and sense of identity—which mutually reinforce one another—are shaped so profoundly by aesthetics, then Christians need to not just participate more frequently in the sacraments but also reflect more deeply on their nature, meaning, and power. When rightly understood, rightly administered, and received with faith, baptism and Communion have the power to shape our self-understanding and moral vision. This is because they connect us to the greatest and most powerful story of all time—the gospel of Jesus Christ. Moreover, the sacraments exhibit the historic church's core beliefs and practices in an attractive and appealing, though certainly ordinary, manner. In baptism and Communion, we find a direct connection between beauty, orthodoxy, and orthopraxy that catechizes the people of God with a greater understanding of the gospel and how they fit into that larger reality as persons in Christ.

The call for renewed and deeper reflection on the sacraments may seem strange or even faddish—especially to "low church" evangelicals who are not formed by a particular confessional heritage and who tend to have a minimalistic view of the sacraments. But the fact is that throughout the history of the church, the sacraments have been integral to Christian life and spirituality. Back in 1977, a group of evangelical theologians emphasized in "The Chicago

---

8 Jonathan Gottschall, *The Storytelling Animal: How Stories Make Us Human* (Boston: Mariner Books, 2013), 152.

9 Charles Taylor, *Sources of the Self: The Making of the Modern Identity* (Cambridge, MA: Harvard University Press, 1989).

Call" a need for modern evangelicals to return to the "historic roots" of the church by not only embracing "the abiding value of the great ecumenical creeds and the Reformation confessions" but also returning to "sacramental integrity" and "a sacramental life." In their call, they decried "the poverty of sacramental understanding among evangelicals," which they said was "largely due to the loss of our continuity with the teaching of many of the Fathers and Reformers." Such loss, they maintained, "results in the deterioration of sacramental life in our churches" and "leads us to disregard the sacredness of daily living."[10] Sadly, "The Chicago Call" has been largely neglected, and our connection with our Christian ancestors and their deep understanding of what it means to be persons in Christ remains largely severed. To return to our historical roots and also understand what it means to be in-Christ persons, we need to embrace a mindset—indeed, a manner of life—that is grounded in and consciously oriented toward the sacraments and specifically the gospel truths they communicate.

The sacraments not only provide continuity with the historic church but—when connected to and given meaning by the written word of God—also give us a clear picture of Christ, what he has done for us, and what it means to be persons in him. A proper understanding of ourselves, therefore, cannot be attained without reflecting deeply on Christ and his body, the church. And the church offers us the greatest and truest story of all. The corporate events of baptism and Communion are a major part of that story because they are integral to the life and identity of the church, and they shape in profound ways our understanding of Christ and his

---

10 "The Chicago Call of 1977," Epiclesis, accessed December 14, 2022, https://www.epiclesis .org/. See also Simon Chan, *Liturgical Theology: The Church as Worshiping Community* (Downers Grove, IL: IVP Academic, 2006), 11.

body, of which we are members, thereby helping us discern ourselves better. And as we immerse ourselves into the gospel story heralded faithfully by the historic church, we come to understand with greater certainty that we are, fundamentally, baptized and communing persons.

One passage in Scripture that, when read canonically and theologically with input from faithful interpreters throughout church history, reinforces the truth that we are baptized and communing persons is John 19:34, which reports that "there came out blood and water" from Christ's side after he was pierced. John Calvin, for one, teaches that the blood and water, the two symbols for sacrifices and washings in the Old Testament, represent atonement and cleansing, justification and sanctification—the chief benefits that Christ has secured for us.[11] And following Augustine,[12] Calvin believes that our sacraments, baptism (washing) and Communion (atonement), represent these benefits and enable us to embrace them more firmly. John Chrysostom, speaking of the water and blood that flowed from Christ's side, says that the church exists by these two.[13] Those who possess faith in Christ are regenerated by water and nourished by his body and blood. Just as Eve was made from the side of Adam, so the church, the bride of Christ,

---

11 John Calvin, *The Gospel according to St. John 11–21 and the First Epistle of John*, ed. David W. Torrance and T. F. Torrance, trans T. H. L Parker, CNTC 5 (Grand Rapids, MI: Eerdmans, 1961), 186.

12 Augustine, *Lectures or Tractates on the Gospel according to St. John*, trans. John Gibb, NPNF[1] 7:434 (120.2).

13 John Chrysostom, *Joannis Chrysostomi Opera Omnia*, ed. J.-P. Migne, PG 59 (Paris, 1862), 463. Not all interpreters see the water and the blood that flowed from Christ's side as symbolic of baptism and Communion. Given how the images of water and blood function in John's Gospel, however, a strong case can be made that the water and the blood from Christ's side not only prove that he was truly human and that he indeed died but also refer to the sacraments, which signify and seal cleansing from sin and guilt, new life and atonement, sanctification and justification. Numerous premodern interpreters of the passage lean in this direction.

is made from the side of Christ.[14] We are persons of the water and the blood, persons who have been cleansed from our sin and guilt and made one with the triune God. Our very existence and identity as Christians are constituted by Christ and his self-giving work of salvation, which are portrayed to us in baptism and Communion.

Moving Forward

Those in positions to catechize and counsel Christians especially should reflect more deeply on the notion that *being in Christ* is our primary identity as Christians. Such church leaders need to be sufficiently equipped to relay to those under their care a proper theological account for understanding their identity as Christians, as baptized and communing persons, which, in turn, ought to give meaning and shape to the more specific elements of their identities as particular persons. Yet my hope is that readers beyond this group embark on this journey as well. Those interested in learning more about the sacraments will find here, I hope, a fresh yet biblically and historically faithful treatment of the sacraments, all told to the view of what they reveal about our status and calling as in-Christ persons. Therefore, this book will also be of interest to those looking to understand more deeply the doctrine of union with Christ.

The first two chapters explore the sacraments in a general manner, laying the groundwork for understanding what the sacraments teach us about being persons in Christ—and indeed, how they form us as persons in Christ. Chapter 1 focuses on the relation between Scripture and sacrament. Chapter 2 discusses the nature and purpose of the sacraments in greater detail and how the sacraments form and shape the people of God.

---

14 Augustine, *Gospel of John*, 434–35 (120.2).

The next two chapters pay special attention to the sacraments themselves and what they show us about Christian identity. Chapters 3 and 4 explore baptism and Communion, respectively, focusing primarily on what they reveal about our identity as persons who have been immersed into Christ and who commune with him. The final two chapters focus on two biblical-theological themes relating to Christian purpose. Chapter 5 explores conformity to Christ, with primary emphasis on Christian morality, and chapter 6 discusses participation in Christ's ministry. As those redeemed, we are called to embrace both his moral vision and his spiritual mission. Thus, chapters 5 and 6 focus more intently on the imperative truths of being in-Christ persons. And the sacraments are ever in focus, for, when connected to the word of God, they present to us what it means to live as persons joined to and commissioned by the Savior.

I intend this book to be confessional-theological. It aims to confess what Holy Scripture teaches about who we are in Christ and to provide a theological account that is informed by faithful, historic Christian dogma. It takes "The Chicago Call" seriously and seeks to help others return to the historical roots of the church by promoting deeper reflection on the sacraments. Every chapter therefore appeals to major historical Protestant confessions and stalwart Christian thinkers who have demonstrated faithful exegesis and fruitful theological reflection. I apply what orthodox Christians have affirmed through the centuries to our current situation, one that is marked by agonizing uncertainty over personal meaning and purpose.

It is imperative that I mention at the outset that I do not intend to address the unique aspects of people's individuality—that is, what makes them persons distinct from others. Features of a person's particularity—from genetic makeup, personality, and family narrative to vocation, education, and hobbies, to name just a few—are not in view in this work. My goal is to speak to the identity that *all Christians* share as in-Christ persons and to show that the sacraments of baptism and Communion provide a robust theological grid for understanding that identity. And it is through this grid that every aspect of our individuality must be discerned. Our primary identity as in-Christ persons is the controlling feature of all other identity markers, and it provides clarity amid confusion and produces joy and hope instead of despair.

With that stated, let us think about what it means to be in Christ and how the sacraments testify to and solidify the identity we have received in him as persons of the water and the blood.

1

Word and Sacrament

MANY CHRISTIANS TODAY have a weak understanding of the sacraments and what they accomplish in the lives of believers. We know they are important because Christ commanded that we observe them, but we are largely ignorant of their purpose and power. Baptism and Communion have existed as long as the church has and are thus integral to the life and identity of the church. They are, as I stated in the introduction, characteristic of the church: they reveal definitive qualities of what the church is, what she believes, and how she acts. If these ancient rites reveal the life and identity of the church, then it is no stretch to say that they reveal something about the particular members of the church. In an age when many Christians, not just people outside the church, are wondering where they can find personal meaning and purpose, clarity and peace and assurance with regard to who they are, the best options lie right before our eyes—literally, in the context of God's people gathered for worship.

To suggest, however, that the sacraments help us become better attuned to what it means to be persons in Christ raises an essential question: What about Scripture? Does not God's written word teach us all we need to know concerning spiritual matters and therefore what being in Christ means for personal identity and purpose?

One of the great legacies of the Protestant Reformation is the recognition of the preeminence of Scripture, that God's written word is the chief source for theological investigation and religious matters, the one to which all others must yield. This is in contrast to the teaching of Roman Catholicism, for example, which ranks Scripture and church tradition so closely that both are deemed equally authoritative. As the Second Vatican Council's document on divine revelation, *Dei Verbum*, declares, "It is not from Sacred Scripture alone that the Church draws her certainty about everything which has been revealed. Therefore both sacred tradition and Sacred Scripture are to be accepted and venerated *with the same sense of loyalty and reverence*."[1] Scripture cannot be rightly understood apart from the equally authoritative magisterium, and the latter is just as necessary as the former for ascertaining divine truth. Protestants say no to this, and doggedly so, as it implies that God's word is insufficient or unclear in what it communicates to God's people. And so we champion *sola Scriptura* (Scripture alone): Scripture, as self-revelation of the triune God—in whom there is no fault or deficiency and who is supremely authoritative as Creator and Redeemer—is the perfect, sufficient, and ultimate authority for the church regarding faith and practice.[2]

So it may seem that our question is already answered and that we ought to redirect our focus: we need not busy ourselves with

---

1 Roman Catholic Church, *Dei Verbum* (1965), Vatican, accessed August 17, 2021, https://www.vatican.va/; emphasis added.

2 I do not offer here a defense of *sola Scriptura* but rather presuppose it. My aim in this chapter is not to prove the authority, sufficiency, validity, or perspicuity of Scripture but to joyfully affirm these traits while discussing the relation between word and sacrament.

discussing the sacraments in attempts to discover what it means to be a person in Christ. Scripture, after all, offers the answers, for it is God's written word, supremely authoritative on spiritual matters.

Yet *sola Scriptura* does not, and never has historically, maintained that other sources have no significance for the task of theology or for the shaping of Christian piety—and therefore for molding our self-consciousness as persons in Christ. *Sola Scriptura*, which maintains that God's written word is the supreme authority in all matters of faith, must not be confused with *nuda Scriptura* (bare Scripture) or *solo Scriptura* (only Scripture), an erroneous and foolish notion that Scripture can be understood outside any ecclesial context or that other sources have no bearing whatsoever on the task of theology, which necessarily informs our manner of living. Never mind that it is impossible to adhere to the idea in practice. Scripture is not the only means through which God nourishes his people and draws them ever closer to himself. That much is affirmed by chief Protestant theologians since Reformation times and by definitive Protestant confessions. And the sacraments in particular have played a significant role in the life of the church, in nourishing God's people. Thus John Calvin says,

> We are assisted by [the sacraments] in cherishing, confirming, and increasing the true knowledge of Christ, so as both to possess him more fully, and enjoy him in all his richness, so far are they effectual in regard to us. This is the case when that which is there offered is received by us in true faith.[3]

Calvin, as ardent a proponent of the Protestant Reformation as any and one who intrepidly chastised Rome for depreciating Scripture,

---

3 John Calvin, *Institutes of the Christian Religion*, ed. John T. McNeill, trans. Ford Lewis Battles (Philadelphia: Westminster John Knox, 1960), 4.14.13 (hereafter cited as *Inst.*).

recognizes that God in Christ by the Spirit strengthens his people by various means—the sacraments being a vital one.

So when it comes to fortifying our understanding of what it means to be a person in Christ, it is detrimental to think along either-or lines, as though we must choose between using either Scripture or the sacraments for theological investigation and spiritual formation. To do so is to misunderstand the nature of both word and sacrament, which are divine gifts, and their relationship to one another. Scripture grounds the sacraments, and the sacraments reinforce or accentuate Scripture; Scripture and sacrament are complementary, not competing, and both offer us *Christ*.[4] As Robert Bruce so wonderfully remarks, there is nothing greater than "to be conjoined with Jesus Christ," and the "two special means" of procuring that "heavenly and celestial conjunction" are the preaching of the word and administration of the sacraments.[5] Both word and sacrament play a vital, complementary role in joining us to Christ, the one in whom we find our identity.

This chapter, therefore, focuses primarily on the means by which God communicates himself to his people and the relationship the sacraments have to the written word. In the next, we examine the nature of the sacraments, though I cannot avoid discussing that in some form here. Once we have laid this groundwork, we will be ready to immerse ourselves into and feast richly on Scripture's teaching on the sacraments and what they communicate to us about Christian identity and purpose.

4 I am indebted to John C. Clark for this expression. See also "Sacraments in Worship," Ligonier, September 15, 2017, https://www.ligonier.org/.

5 Robert Bruce, *The Mystery of the Lord's Supper: Sermons on the Sacrament Preached in the Kirk of Edinburgh in A.D. 1589 by Robert Bruce*, trans. and ed. Thomas F. Torrance (London: James Clarke, 1958), 39.

Properties of the Word

A good first step to take in understanding the relation between word and sacrament is knowing the nature or characteristics of the word of God, particularly what the principle of *sola Scriptura* affirms. This is because Scripture is the necessary grounding for the sacraments. The sacraments have no meaning apart from the word. So to understand the sacraments aright and what they reveal about our identity as in-Christ persons, we must first understand Scripture, the ultimate authority on matters of faith.

The most fundamental reason that Scripture is the ultimate authority on matters of faith is that it is God's self-revelation, or self-communication.[6] Scripture is not fundamentally about human beings and therefore is not primarily a cultic or ethics manual, though it does reveal a great deal about who we are and how God would have his people worship and live to him. Scripture is principally God's revelation of himself, who he is and what he has done and does, as well as who he is in relation to his creation. It is not primarily an anthropocentric or anthropological book but a theocentric and theological one—it is the word *about* God. And as God's revelation of himself, Scripture is *from* God. He is both the main content and primary origin of Scripture—as well as its end goal. Scripture is supremely both about him and from him, and it leads us to him so that we may know and enjoy him more deeply and intimately.

As the apostle Paul writes, "All Scripture is breathed out by God and profitable for teaching, for reproof, for correction, and for training in righteousness, that the man of God may be complete,

---

6 See John Webster, *Holy Scripture: A Dogmatic Sketch*, Current Issues in Theology (Cambridge: Cambridge University Press, 2003), 5–17.

equipped for every good work" (2 Tim. 3:16–17). All, every bit—the seemingly mundane or obscure, as well as the recognizably exhilarating and profound, every word and not just the parts we prefer—is exhaled by God. Or as the apostle Peter states, the writings of Scripture are the product of men being "carried along by the Holy Spirit" (2 Pet. 1:21). So while the human authors worked in their own particular ways and communicated with their own unique styles and voices, what they produced was not conjured of their own wills. They were guided by God's Spirit in such a way that they may be truly called authors, not amanuenses, though God is the originator of the content they produced. This is what is affirmed by the doctrine of the inspiration of Scripture, God working through human authors and messengers to reveal himself and his purposes.

Already we come to grasp a little of who we are: creatures made to know God. He wants to communicate, indeed give, himself to us. He has deemed us worthy, not because of some inherent virtue within us but because of his unconditional love and supreme grace, to be recipients of his self-revelation. He has breathed out to us his word about himself so that we may be filled with his very life and enjoy eternal fellowship with him. And he has chosen to use humans in the process. He has deemed us fitting agents for divine communication. We are, as beings made in his image, given unrivaled dignity.

Because Scripture is God-breathed, exhaled by the triune God, who alone is perfect and without error, it is completely trustworthy as "the principal guide and leader unto all godliness and virtue."[7] Scripture is true and reliable, without fault, not because of the human authors but because of who God is. Irenaeus wrote in the

---

7   The 1547 and 1562 prefaces to the First Book of Homilies in *The Books of Homilies: A Critical Edition*, ed. Gerald Bray (Cambridge: James Clark, 2015), 3, 5.

second century, "The Scriptures are indeed perfect, since they were spoken by the Word of God and His Spirit."[8] And the Homilies of the Church of England express, "It cannot therefore be but truth which proceedeth from the God of all truth."[9] It seems impossible that words written and transmitted by sinful humans could be wholly truthful and without fault. Yet the old expression holds true here: God can use a crooked stick to draw a straight line. The human authors, though imperfect in themselves, were used by God, carried along by his Spirit, in such a way that the autographs are dependable guides to truth. As the Westminster divines affirm, "The authority of the Holy Scripture, for which it ought to be believed and obeyed, dependent not upon the testimony of any man, or Church; but wholly upon God (who is truth itself) the author thereof: and therefore it is to be received because it is the Word of God."[10] God in his perfection is able to preserve the integrity and sanctity of his word.

Scripture is also perspicuous, or clear. Our all-wise and all-powerful God both knows how and is able to communicate in such a manner that his revelation of himself is intelligible to humans. God is indeed beyond comprehension, as the prophet Isaiah poignantly captures:

For as the heavens are higher than the earth,
    so are my ways higher than your ways
    and my thoughts than your thoughts. (Isa. 55:9)

---

8   Irenaeus, *Against Heresies*, in *ANF* 1:399 (2.28.2).
9   "An Information for Them Which Take Offence at Certain Places of Holy Scripture," in Bray, *Books of Homilies*, 373.
10 Westminster Confession of Faith 1.4 (hereafter cited as WCF), in *Creeds, Confessions, and Catechisms: A Reader's Edition*, ed. Chad Van Dixhoorn (Wheaton, IL: Crossway, 2022), 184 (hereafter cited as *CCC*).

But the fact that God is mysterious and incomprehensible, dwelling in unapproachable light (1 Tim. 6:16), does not mean he has chosen to remain hidden from us. He has revealed himself to us in his word—and ultimately in his Son incarnate, Jesus Christ. This act of revealing himself to us Calvin calls *accommodation*, God's condescending to our level so that we may understand and know him. Scripture, then, is like the "lisping" of a nurse to an infant, Calvin explains.[11] Baby talk may seem an offensive analogy to draw when explaining God's communication to us, but it suggests tender affection and eagerness to bond by any means possible. Scripture is God's meeting us where we are, his communication to us in terms and concepts we are able to understand. While God may be too lofty for us to ascend to him by reason, he is not too lofty to stoop to us, and Scripture is a primary means by which God has descended to us. It is his way of speaking in layman's terms, as it were.

This, however, does not mean that all parts of Scripture are "alike plain in themselves, nor alike clear unto all."[12] Many passages are difficult to understand, but "that is due, not to any lack of clarity in Scripture," Martin Luther explains, "but to [our] own blindness and dullness, in that [we] make no effort to see truth which, in itself, could not be plainer."[13] The problems we experience result from our own limitations or obduracy rather than any inherent fault in God's word.

So, returning to the pronouncements of Westminster, to say that Scripture is perspicuous or clear is to affirm that "those things which are necessary to be known, believed, and observed for salvation, are

11 Calvin, *Inst.*, 1.13.1.
12 WCF 1.7 (*CCC* 186).
13 Martin Luther, *The Bondage of the Will: A New Translation of "De Servo Arbitrio" (1525); Martin Luther's Reply to Erasmus of Rotterdam*, trans. J. I. Packer and O. R. Johnston (London: James Clarke, 1957), 72.

so clearly propounded and opened in some place of Scripture or other, that not only the learned, but the unlearned, in a due use of the ordinary means, may attain unto a sufficient understanding of them."[14] Yet this does not suggest that we are capable of understanding Scripture on our own apart from divine assistance. We may be creatures of supreme dignity, but we are sinful and need divine illumination, the act whereby the Spirit of God scatters the darkness from our hearts and minds so that we may discern his truth. This is what Paul gets at when he insists that the things of God are "spiritually discerned" (1 Cor. 2:14). No one, he exclaims, "comprehends the thoughts of God except the Spirit of God" (1 Cor. 2:11). The "natural person," the one alienated from Christ and yet to be regenerated by the Spirit, "does not accept the things of the Spirit of God" (1 Cor. 2:14). Only the "spiritual person," the one whom the Spirit indwells and animates, has "the mind of Christ" (1 Cor. 2:16) and is able to interpret "spiritual truths" (1 Cor. 2:13). So while Scripture is plain and clear regarding what is necessary for salvation, these truths, along with all the riches of Scripture, can be embraced only when the Spirit of God enables a person to do so. The Spirit of God and the word of God cannot be separated. The key to grasping the truth of Scripture, in a way that leads to life and blessedness, is *Spiritus cum verbo*, the Spirit working with the word.[15] The Spirit is always connected to the word. He is the agent of inspiration and illumination. And because the Spirit, the Lord and giver of life—to use the description of the Niceno-Constantinopolitan Creed—is always working through the word, the word is "living and active" (Heb. 4:12). It is not an antiquated document or inert

---

14 WCF 1.7 (*CCC* 186).

15 Richard B. Gaffin Jr., *In the Fullness of Time: An Introduction to the Biblical Theology of Acts and Paul* (Wheaton, IL: Crossway, 2022), 152.

object but an animate and mighty tool in the hands of the living God that accomplishes his purposes of revelation and redemption. God's written word faithfully testifies to the living Word, Jesus Christ, communicating clearly to us all that God deemed necessary for us to know for the salvation attained by him, and therefore, it is sufficient—for knowing, trusting, loving, and obeying Christ, its supreme subject. No other means is required for attaining a knowledge of true religion. "There is no truth nor doctrine necessary for our justification and everlasting salvation but that is, or may be, drawn out of that fountain and well of truth," as the Homilies puts it. "In Holy Scripture is fully contained what we ought to do and what to eschew, what to believe, what to love and what to look for at God's hands at length."[16] Or as the Thirty-Nine Articles proclaims, "Holy Scripture containeth all things necessary to salvation: so that whatsoever is not read therein, nor may be proved thereby, is not to be required of any man, that it should be believed as an article of the Faith, or be thought requisite or necessary to salvation."[17] This conviction is not peculiar to a single stream of Protestant thought but distinguishes Protestantism from any tradition that deems Scripture wanting. The Belgic Confession declares, "We believe that this Holy Scripture contains the will of God completely and that everything one must believe to be saved is sufficiently taught in it."[18] And the Westminster divines agree:

> The whole counsel of God concerning all things necessary for his own glory, man's salvation, faith and life, is either expressly set down in Scripture, or by good and necessary consequence

16 "A Fruitful Exhortation to the Reading of Holy Scripture," in Bray, *Books of Homilies*, 7.
17 Thirty-Nine Articles, art. 6 (*CCC* 116).
18 Belgic Confession, art. 7 (*CCC* 82).

may be deduced from Scripture: unto which nothing at any time is to be added, whether by new revelations of the Spirit, or traditions of men.[19]

As John Yates III rightly explains, "To speak of the sufficiency of Scripture is both an affirmation and a qualification. It is entirely sufficient for redemption but not exhaustive concerning everything in life."[20] While Scripture is not limited in the sense that it is faulty or weak, it is limited in its focus, dealing with specific rather than all matters—yet in what it focuses on, it is completely authoritative and true and so is a reliable guide to salvation and the life lived by faith.

Because of these characteristics, God's word is "a sure, steadfast and everlasting instrument of salvation," as stated in the Homilies.[21] It is the primary channel through which our triune God communicates himself and his deeds to his people—in such a way that grace is conferred when the Spirit of God is animate within believers, granting faith in the promises of God. Scripture is "living and active" (Heb. 4:12), operating on our hearts and minds; it grants us life (Ps. 119:25, 50, 93, 107, 154, 156); it is a lamp to our feet and a light to our path (Ps. 119:105); it accomplishes God's purposes, going out from him without returning to him void (Isa. 55:11); it is not bound (2 Tim. 2:9). God's written word is an effective means through which he produces spiritual life in believers when his Spirit, who illuminates them and leads them to faith, indwells and quickens them.

---

19 WCF 1.6 (*CCC* 186).
20 John W. Yates III, "*Sola Scriptura*," in *Reformation Anglicanism: A Vision for Today's Global Communion*, ed. Ashley Null and John W. Yates III (Wheaton, IL: Crossway, 2017), 83.
21 "A Fruitful Exhortation to the Reading of Holy Scripture," in Bray, *Books of Homilies*, 8.

Additions to the Word

To say that Scripture alone is the perfect, sufficient, and final authority regarding faith and practice and that it is an instrument by which God produces life within believers when his Spirit illuminates them and leads them to faith does not mean that it is the only means by which God makes himself known. The classic distinction between so-called general and specific, or natural and supernatural, revelation serves the point. As the Belgic Confession states, "We know God by two means: First, by the creation, preservation, and government of the universe," and second, "by his holy and divine Word."[22] In the created order, history, and humanity, God reveals general truths about himself that all people, whether regenerated by the Spirit or not, are able to discern.

Scripture itself, in both the Old and New Testaments, testifies that God has disclosed himself in the universe. As the psalmist rejoices,

> The heavens declare the glory of God,
>   and the sky above proclaims his handiwork.
> Day to day pours out speech,
>   and night to night reveals knowledge. (Ps. 19:1–2)

Perhaps Paul had this passage in mind when he exclaimed, "For his invisible attributes, namely, his eternal power and divine nature, have been clearly perceived, ever since the creation of the world, in the things that have been made." For this reason, we are "without excuse" if we do not acknowledge that God exists (Rom. 1:20) and therefore reckoned fools (Ps. 14:1). The created order will not permit us to plead agnosticism.

22 Belgic Confession, art. 2 (CCC 79).

Calvin, for one, reiterates these sorts of truths when he speaks of creation as a reflection of divine glory and power. The universe, in its splendor and "artistic construction," is so "skillfully ordered" that it is "for us a sort of mirror in which we can contemplate God, who is otherwise invisible."[23] Since all creation displays "those immense riches of [God's] wisdom, justice, goodness and power," Calvin urges, "we should not merely run over them cursorily, and immediately forget about them; but we should ponder them at length, turn them over in our minds seriously and faithfully, and recollect them repeatedly."[24] And even the constitution of human nature "presents a very clear mirror of God's work," particularly his governance. This truth is seen in many ways, Calvin explains, especially in infants who, as "they nurse at their mother's breasts, have tongues so eloquent to preach his glory that there is no need at all of other orators."[25]

Simply put, when we pause to meditate on the natural world and even ourselves, we should immediately "ponder the invisible things of God: his eternal power and divinity," as the Belgic Confession states, appealing to Romans 1:20.[26]

Yet these truths, if recognized, do not lead to a saving knowledge of the triune God, though they do lead us to knowledge of our guilt before him. The created order, history, and humanity are limited insofar as they communicate that an all-powerful God, who created all things, exists and governs our world. But they do not reveal God's plan of redemption, which culminates in the person and work of Jesus Christ. Thus the necessity of special revelation, "God's manifestation *of himself* to particular persons at definite

23 Calvin, *Inst.*, 1.5.1.
24 Calvin, *Inst.*, 1.14.21.
25 Calvin, *Inst.*, 1.5.3.
26 Belgic Confession, art. 2 (*CCC* 79).

times and places, enabling those persons to enter into a redemptive relationship with him."²⁷ God has made himself known in certain historical events (which are different in nature from human history in general), in divine speech, and ultimately in the incarnation of his Son. It is through these that God has manifested himself more fully to humanity so that we may be reconciled to him. And all three types of particular revelation are recorded in Scripture, meaning that Scripture may truly be called divine revelation because "it is an accurate reproduction of the original revelation."²⁸ It may also be called revelation because God's Spirit guided the human authors in the writing of the Scriptures. The Gospels, for instance, do not simply *contain* revelation, in that they record certain original, revelatory acts and teachings of Jesus Christ, the incarnate Son of God, but also *are revelation* because the Holy Spirit superintended the writing of each narrative, including the wording and form of each. All Scripture is breathed out by God.

So to attain a saving knowledge of the triune God, we must turn to Holy Scripture, by which God "makes himself known to us more openly."²⁹ And as Scripture leads us into a fuller knowledge of God as Redeemer, it also equips us to rightly discern God's glory in creation, history, and humanity. To use Calvin's metaphor, the Scriptures are the "spectacles" or lens through which we must look, with eyes of faith, in order to behold all things clearly.³⁰

With these profound truths established and affirmed, we return to our initial questions: Does not Scripture sufficiently communicate all matters pertaining to faith and practice? Is it not the

27 Millard J. Erickson, *Christian Theology*, 3rd ed. (Grand Rapids, MI: Baker Academic, 2003), 144; emphasis added.
28 Erickson, *Christian Theology*, 163.
29 Belgic Confession, art. 2 (*CCC* 79).
30 Calvin, *Inst.*, 1.6.1; 1.14.1.

ultimate *regula fidei* (rule of faith), the standard for religious belief? And more particularly, does it not successfully relay what it means to be a person in Christ and what union with him means for personal identity and existence? The answers are incontrovertibly yes, lest we infer that Scripture itself, as revelation from the Father that proceeds through the Son and by the agency of the Holy Spirit, is defective. God's word is clear, reliable, sufficient, authoritative, and effective—and we may heartily rejoice in that glorious truth.

Yet God, as a compassionate, attentive Father who knows that we are formed from dust (Ps. 103:13–14), is "mindful of our crudeness and weakness."[31] And mindful of our creaturely condition, he has deemed it fitting to make himself knowable and accessible through various means, through what many theologians over the centuries have termed "means of grace" (*media gratiae*). Considering the goodness of God and his endless delight in expressing himself to his people, Stephen Charnock writes,

All goodness delights to communicate itself. Infinite goodness has then an infinite delight in expressing itself; it is a part of his goodness not to be weary of showing it. He can never then be weary of being solicited for the effusions of it. If he rejoices over his people to do them good, he will rejoice in any opportunities offered to him to honor his goodness and gladly meet with a fit object for it.[32]

Though these words appear in a discussion on prayer rather than on the sacraments, they nevertheless reinforce the truth that God

31 Belgic Confession, art. 33 (*CCC* 105).
32 Stephen Charnock, *The Existence and Attributes of God: Updated and Unabridged*, ed. Mark Jones, vol. 2 (Wheaton, IL: Crossway, 2022), 1361.

takes immense pleasure in extending his goodness to those who seek him—and that he takes any opportunity to do so. This passage also employs the concept of "fittingness": that God sees it fit or suitable, though not necessary as if he were bound, to act in the manner he has and to use certain means in communicating himself and his goodness to his people. Like any good parent, God is delighted to bestow on his children diverse gifts so that they may know him as a loving Father and be blessed by him. He is so paternally indulgent, so affectionately generous, that he has given us multiple means whereby we may perceive his glory and goodness and thus fortify our faith and grow in our delight in him. And one reason God gives us such a variety of gifts—especially tangible gifts such as the sacraments—is because we are spiritual-physical beings created with multiple senses. It is therefore fitting or proper that God should use various means to engage our entire beings.

Scripture is, as I have already indicated, a means of grace in that it generates and promotes faith and grants spiritual blessings to those whom the Spirit illuminates and leads to divine truth. It guides us in the way of life. Scripture, as divine speech communicated by the triune God, is adapted to our hearing, and it is through hearing the word of God that we come to faith in Christ (Rom. 10:14–17). And as it creates and strengthens faith within us, it targets our intellects, affections, and imaginations. To be sure, Scripture, God's written word, also appeals to our eyes in some manner as we read it. This means that while God's word engages our hearing and also, to some extent, our sight, the rest of our senses are left unengaged. This does not mean, however, that Scripture is defective in any sense but that it targets a particular sensual aspect of our being. For this reason, as the Belgic Confession asserts, "God has added [the sacraments] to the Word of the gospel to represent better to our external senses both what God enables us to understand by the Word and what he does inwardly in our hearts, confirming in us the salvation he imparts to us."[33] The sacraments, therefore, are also rightly called means of grace, for God has deemed them suitable instruments through which he communicates to us the benefits of Christ's redemptive-historical work.[34]

In discussions of the means of grace, it is common to find theologians asserting that God created humans to obtain knowledge of spiritual truths through two primary senses, hearing and sight, and that it is to these two senses that the word and sacraments appeal, respectively.[35] This is certainly true, and I dare not deny it since it is a conviction found early in church history; the fourth-century theologian Augustine, bishop of Hippo, describes the sacraments as visible words—that is, images of the gospel.[36] Yet we may fairly say that the sacraments appeal also to our senses of touch, smell, and taste. As we are plunged into or doused with the waters of baptism, or as we witness others undergo that rite and thus recall our own baptism; as we hold the bread, taste the grain, and then feel that morsel disintegrate in our mouths while we chew; and as

---

33 Belgic Confession, art. 33 (*CCC* 105). Cf. Louis Berkhof, *Systematic Theology*, 4th ed. (Grand Rapids, MI: Eerdmans, 1941), 616; Bruce, *Mystery of the Lord's Supper*, 39–40; W. H. Griffith Thomas, *The Principles of Theology: An Introduction to the Thirty-Nine Articles* (London: Longmans, Green, 1930), 343.

34 E.g., Westminster Shorter Catechism q. 88 (hereafter cited as WSC) (*CCC* 429), and Thirty-Nine Articles, art. 25 (*CCC* 125). Some Protestant confessions and theologians include prayer along with the word and sacraments as the "ordinary means of grace."

35 E.g., Berkhof, *Systematic Theology*, 616; Geerhardus Vos, *Reformed Dogmatics: A System of Christian Theology*, single-vol. ed., trans. and ed. Richard B. Gaffin Jr. (Bellingham, WA: Lexham, 2020), 933.

36 Augustine, *Lectures or Tractates on the Gospel according to St. John*, trans. John Gibb, *NPNF*[1] 7:344 (80.3); cf. Augustine, *Contra Faustum*, trans. Richard Stothert, *NPNF*[1] 4:244 (19.16).

we smell the vigor of the wine[37] and feel it warm our throats as we swallow, we experience the gospel in ways that engage our whole beings—and in ways we cannot by simply hearing or reading.[38]

But somehow, many of us, especially evangelicals not molded by a particular historical confessional heritage, have either lost or never developed our senses of sight, touch, smell, and taste, so to speak. Part of this is due to (rightful) rejection of the sacramental system of Roman Catholicism, in which the so-called seven sacraments are deemed efficacious regardless of whether faith is operative in the recipient. Part of it is due to inherited convictions of Pietism, a movement that emerged within seventeenth-century German Lutheranism and has had considerable influence on American evangelicalism. As R. Scott Clark explains, the movement perceived a cold confessionalism within Lutheranism that stressed correct dogma to the point of depreciating Christian living, and so the movement emphasized vibrant personal faith and experience. This is why in many evangelical circles today, personal spiritual disciplines have supplanted communal celebration of the

37 To be sure, not all Christian traditions use wine in celebration of the Supper and instead opt for grape juice. And not all who participate in this meal should partake of alcoholic wine due to either age, matters of conscience, or a history of addiction. For these reasons, churches that serve wine should also serve juice. As I explain later in this chapter, God is not bound to the sacraments. He can work in and through wine or juice. Nevertheless, I believe something greater is signified in wine than in juice, as is apparent in my discussion of wine and the elevating nature of Christ's work in chap. 4. Not only that, the use of wine accords better with the Passover meal and therefore our Lord's institution of the Supper.

38 Cf. Tim Chester, *Truth We Can Touch: How Baptism and Communion Shape Our Lives* (Wheaton, IL: Crossway, 2020), 39–40. Commenting on the liturgical nature of Reformation Anglicanism, Ashley Null and John Yates explain, "For Cranmer, the sacraments were the ultimate example of the power of God's Word at work. Since human beings learn by their senses—by what they see, hear, smell, taste, and touch—Cranmer believed that when God's Word was joined to creaturely things like water, bread, and wine, the truth of his promises would more deeply impact people." Ashley Null and John W. Yates III, "A Manifesto for Reformation Anglicanism," in Null and Yates, *Reformation Anglicanism*, 199.

sacraments.[39] Another reason why the doctrine of the means of grace is forgotten or rejected by many of us today is that we are heirs of Enlightenment thinking, which prioritizes reason as the ultimate basis for knowing truth and reality. As a result, many people in our modern culture, even Christians, tend to dismiss the significance of physical objects—which is perhaps ironic, given the triumph of materialism. Never mind that the concept of natural law is almost totally forgotten or rejected. Simply put, ours is a day when matter does not matter, even for many Christians. The cumulative effect of these factors, among many potential others, means that many Christians are wary of classifying the sacraments as means of grace, instruments through which God makes himself known and communicates his goodness to us. Both experientialism and rationalism neglect the physical, tangible, touchable elements of the gospel. Both are less than full-bodied understandings of the gospel and so offer truncated versions of the Lord Jesus Christ, who is both fully God and fully human, who is fully bodied, the one in whom our very being and identity is constituted.[40]

Scripture itself, which we so highly cherish, testifies that God uses physical, visible objects to communicate truths about him and his actions or to work on behalf of his people. In the Old Testament alone, we learn that God used water to judge rebellious humanity and to save Noah and his family. He used circumcision to seal (confirm) the righteousness that Abraham had received by faith (Gen. 17; Rom. 4:11), and he used the circumcision of infants to maintain his covenant with Israel and to incorporate

---

39 R. Scott Clark, "The Evangelical Fall from the Means of Grace: The Lord's Supper," in *The Compromised Church: The Present Evangelical Crisis*, ed. John H. Armstrong (Wheaton, IL: Crossway, 1998), 133–47.

40 The substance of these last two sentences was informed by a personal conversation with John C. Clark.

children into his covenant people. When the Feast of Unleavened Bread was established, the Lord said to Moses that "it shall be to you as a sign on your hand and as a memorial between your eyes, that the law of the LORD may be in your mouth." It was to be a reminder to God's people that "with a strong hand the LORD has brought you out of Egypt" (Ex. 13:9–10). He used the cloud by day and the pillar of fire by night to protect and guide the people of Israel once they had left that house of bondage. After Joshua led the people across the Jordan, the Lord instructed him to select twelve elders to set up twelve stones on the dry land as a reminder "that the waters of the Jordan were cut off before the ark of the covenant of the LORD. When it passed over the Jordan, the waters of the Jordan were cut off" (Josh. 4:6–7). And then there are the many sacrifices that God used for the forgiveness of sins when his people turned to him, trusting in him alone.

The list could go on, and this is the world in which the church was born and the New Testament written. So to resist the idea that God uses physical means to extend his goodness and communicate himself to his people is to reject a thoroughly biblical concept. More problematic, the largely nonsacramental tendency of many modern evangelicals is likely the result of forgetting "our confession of the ultimate visible sign of the ultimate invisible reality, failing to embrace the Christ-mystery behind the sacraments."[41] The incarnation itself proves that God joins "himself to us through created, physical, material means, namely, the humanity of his Son. And it is none other than the Son who gives us the holy mysteries of word, water, bread, and wine to bring us the salvation that he is."[42]

41 John C. Clark and Marcus Peter Johnson, *The Incarnation of God: The Mystery of the Gospel as the Foundation of Evangelical Theology* (Wheaton, IL: Crossway, 2015), 192.
42 Clark and Johnson, *Incarnation of God*, 192.

It is imperative to note that the means of grace, the "benefits of redemption," as the Westminster Shorter Catechism teaches, are effectual to the "elect," who have "faith in Jesus Christ, repentance unto life."[43] Moreover, the sacraments are effectual not because of "any virtue in them" or in the person administering them "but only by the blessing of Christ, and the working of his Spirit in them that by faith receive them."[44] The sacraments of baptism and Communion are indeed means of grace, effectual in communicating Christ's redemptive benefits, because they are instruments used by the Spirit of God, who creates within believers faith in the crucified and risen Christ.

Complementary Pictures of the Word

At this point, it is necessary to qualify and elaborate on the nature of both the word and the sacraments, as well as on their relation to each other. The statement needs to be iterated again and perhaps more overtly: the sacraments do not stand on equal footing with Scripture. As the Belgic Confession states, the sacraments are "added" to the word.[45] There is a proper ordering of the two, with Scripture taking priority. Certainly, the word and the sacraments share similarities, yet they also differ significantly, and these differences testify to the superiority of Scripture.[46]

As for the similarities, God is the author of both the word and the sacraments. Just as he is the ultimate origin and primary author of Scripture, so he is the author of and primary agent in

---

43 WSC q. 88, q. 85 (*CCC* 429).
44 WSC q. 91 (*CCC* 430).
45 Belgic Confession, art. 33 (*CCC* 105).
46 Much of what follows is dependent on Vos, *Reformed Dogmatics*, 934–35, whose explanation reflects a traditional Reformed understanding of the sacraments and their relation to the word.

the sacraments, the one who has instituted them through his Son, Jesus Christ, and uses them according to his purpose. It is also imperative to understand that the content of the sacraments and Scripture is the same: *Christ is the main subject matter of both.*[47] As Robert Bruce states, "We get no other thing in the Sacrament than we get in the Word. . . . You get the same thing [in the Sacrament] which you get in the Word."[48] Not only that, the manner in which both are received is the same. Only *by faith* are the word and the sacraments effectual. Without faith, we cannot enjoy Christ, who is present to us in both the word and the sacraments by the power of God's Spirit.

Yet the two differ in ways that should not be overlooked. First, as Geerhardus Vos explains, "The Word is absolutely necessary; the sacraments are not absolutely necessary. Expressed otherwise: the necessity of the latter does not lie on the side of God but on the side of man."[49] Scripture is entirely sufficient for communicating to us all we need to know for salvation. Thus, as Calvin declares, "It is an error to suppose that *anything more* is conferred by the sacraments than is offered by the word of God, and obtained by true faith."[50] While the word is absolutely necessary for salvation—for "faith comes from hearing, and hearing through the word of Christ" (Rom. 10:17)—and while no one can come to a true and saving knowledge of our triune God apart from the word, the sacraments are not absolutely necessary for salvation. Thus we see the difference between *necessity of means* and *necessity of precept.* The sacraments are not necessary *means* for salvation because a person can be saved by

47 Vos, *Reformed Dogmatics*, 934.
48 Bruce, *Mystery of the Lord's Supper*, 84–85.
49 Vos, *Reformed Dogmatics*, 935.
50 Calvin, *Inst.*, 4.14.14; emphasis added.

Christ without them. Yet they are necessary *precepts* (or "*generally necessary* to salvation," as the Anglican catechism *To Be a Christian* puts it)[51] because Christ commanded that we observe them and because he works generally through these ordained means.[52] We are bound to them, though God is not, because Christ has instituted them for our use and benefit.

The word and sacraments also differ in their purpose. Related to the previous point regarding necessity, the word serves *to produce faith*—again, faith comes by hearing the word of Christ—and the sacraments serve *to fortify faith*.[53] This means that the extent of each is also different. The word of God is for all people indiscriminately, regardless of whether they are regenerated and enfolded into God's covenant people. The sacraments, however, are reserved for those who belong to God's new covenant people, for they serve to confirm and strengthen the faith of those incorporated into Christ.

Finally, the word and the sacraments differ in manner of expression, as we have already acknowledged. "The truth addressed to the ear in the Word," Louis Berkhof explains, "is symbolically represented to the eye in the sacraments." This means—and it should not be neglected—that "while the Word can exist and is also complete without the sacraments, the sacraments are never complete without the Word."[54] The sacraments as visible words—a truth that we explore in greater detail in the next chapter and that is foundational to what follows in the remainder of our study—have no meaning

---

51 *To Be a Christian: An Anglican Catechism; Approved Edition*, ed. J. I. Packer and Joel Scandrett (Wheaton, IL: Crossway, 2020), 56; emphasis added.
52 On the distinction between necessity of means and necessity of precept, see Robert Letham, *Systematic Theology* (Wheaton, IL: Crossway, 2019), 646.
53 E.g., Belgic Confession, art. 35 (*CCC* 107); Calvin, *Inst.*, 4.14; Vos, *Reformed Dogmatics*, 935.
54 Berkhof, *Systematic Theology*, 616.

apart from Scripture. As Vos helpfully puts it, "The Word is resident in the sacrament. The Word is accompanied with the sacrament. If one takes away the Word, there is nothing left of the sacrament. If one takes away the sacrament, because of that the Word is still not lost."[55] Again, Scripture grounds the sacraments.

And so I reiterate what I stated at the outset of this chapter: When it comes to understanding more firmly who we are in Christ, what being united to him means for personal identity and purpose, we do not need to take an either-or approach. We are not faced with turning to either Scripture or the sacraments. Because the content of both the word and the sacraments is the same—namely, Christ and his saving work—everything that I propose we draw from the sacraments is in fact drawn from Scripture itself, though the sacraments communicate these truths *in multisensory form*. And so the sacraments punctuate Scripture. The sacraments are visible words, physical representations of the gospel. Scripture and the sacraments are complementary and do not compete with one another. And as is evident in subsequent chapters, the sacraments summarize various teachings about Christ, his work, and what it means to be united to and abide in him. Put differently, the sacraments are pregnant with gospel truths, about both Christ and us as members of his body, that God wishes to deliver to his people so that they may be nourished to everlasting life.

As Sinclair Ferguson explains, "We do not get a different or a better Christ in the sacraments than we do in the word. . . . But we may get the same Christ better, with a firmer grasp of his grace through seeing, touching, feeling, and tasting as well as hearing."[56]

---

55 Vos, *Reformed Dogmatics*, 934.
56 Sinclair B. Ferguson, *The Whole Christ: Legalism, Antinomianism, and Gospel Assurance; Why the Marrow Controversy Still Matters* (Wheaton, IL: Crossway, 2016), 223.

Or as Calvin provocatively states, "The sacraments bring *the clearest promises*; and they have this characteristic over and above the word because they represent them for us as painted in a picture from life."[57] Moreover, through the sacraments, "God attests his good will and love toward us more expressly than by word."[58] They make God's word "more evident" and "more certain."[59] And Bruce adds,

> That same thing which you possess by the hearing of the Word, you now possess more fully. God has more room in your soul, through your receiving of the Sacrament, than he could otherwise have by your hearing of the Word only. What then, you ask, is the new thing we get? *We get Christ better than we did before.* We get the thing which we had more fully, that is, with a surer apprehension than we had before. We get a better grip of Christ now, for by the Sacrament my faith is nourished, the bounds of my soul are enlarged, and so where I had but a little grip of Christ before, as it were, between my finger and my thumb, now I get Him in my whole hand, and indeed the more my faith grows, the better grip I get of Christ Jesus. Thus the Sacrament is very necessary, if only for the reason that we get Christ better, and get a firmer grasp of Him by the Sacrament than we could have before.[60]

Stalwart Protestant theologians have affirmed that the sacraments give us the same thing we get by hearing the word of God but better, enabling us to draw nearer to Christ and embrace him

57 Calvin, *Inst.*, 4.14.5; emphasis added.
58 Calvin, *Inst.*, 4.14.6.
59 Calvin, *Inst.*, 4.14.3, 6. See also Chester, *Truth We Can Touch*, 39.
60 Bruce, *Mystery of the Lord's Supper*, 84–85; emphasis added.

more firmly. Similarly, the sacraments do not present to us a different or better teaching on what it means to be persons in Christ than what Scripture offers us, but we may grasp the same teaching more fully and firmly by giving greater attention and adherence to the sacraments, for they appeal to our entire being, delighting all our senses.

To affirm that the sacraments help us attain a firmer grasp of what it means to be a person in Christ, to understand more fully what it means to have our life constituted in him, does not suggest that we depart from hallmark Protestant convictions. Rather, it honors the Reformation heritage by affirming the conviction that the sacraments strengthen our faith and understanding of the triune God whom we worship and serve. The Reformation tradition resolutely affirms *sola Scriptura* while simultaneously recognizing that Scripture is but one of the means, though certainly the chief, through which our triune God works to make himself known and communicate his goodness to us. Some questions still need to be answered before we turn our attention to baptism and Communion in particular, questions that lead us to consider in more detail the nature of the sacraments and why they are considered means of grace—and how they could possibly teach us and form us as in-Christ persons. And so it is to those questions that we turn in the next chapter.

2

Sacraments and Identity

THE SACRAMENTS, MUCH LIKE the issue of personal identity, are subject to debate and confusion. Numerous catechisms ask, "What is a sacrament?"—a question that leads some Christians to enter into intense theological and pastoral disputes and causes others to recoil in fear of appearing ignorant or of potentially offending those who hold divergent opinions. Still others apply their own personal understanding to these ancient rites while disregarding how Christians of past generations have understood and practiced them. If we wish to see clearly the connection between the sacraments and Christian identity, we must get clear on what the sacraments are. Before we are able to explore in detail *what* the sacraments teach us about being in-Christ persons, we must first understand *how* they are able to teach us—and indeed form us. We have already discovered that the sacraments are sources of revelation—alongside though never instead of or above Scripture—means through which God communicates his love and goodness to his children. In this chapter, we shift our focus slightly to consider additional though related features of the sacraments, features that help us see more clearly how baptism and Communion are able to declare what it means to be in Christ and to shape us into persons who become like him.

We will also, I pray, come to understand more deeply the importance of listening to the historic church. The Christian faith is received or inherited, passed down from generation to generation, meaning that one does not come to faith in the crucified and risen Lord in isolation from others. This statement alone has profound implications for understanding Christian identity, both what it means to be in Christ and what union with him means for our existence as particular persons. We do not, and cannot, exist as autonomous beings capable of determining on our own what is true—either about God and his creation or about ourselves individually. To acquire an understanding of the truth, about any subject matter, requires us to be connected to others and to receive from them. This is true for, say, grasping a language or understanding mathematics, and it is no less true for coming to faith in Christ and attaining maturity in him. The Christian faith was "once for all delivered to the saints" (Jude 3), and the church, including all her members, is built on the foundation of the apostles and the prophets, with Christ being the cornerstone (Eph. 2:20).

The sacraments reinforce the truth that we belong to a collective, to Christ *and his body*. We are, to use another biblical metaphor, branches joined not just to the vine but also to other branches stemming from our Lord. To use sacramental language, we are baptized (or immersed) into Christ, and we commune with the triune God and one another by virtue of our union with the Son. The sacraments are also rites characteristic of the catholic or universal church, practices that reveal definitive qualities of who she is, what she believes, and what she does. The cumulative effect of these truths should therefore cause us to acknowledge that if we wish to understand more deeply who we are, and if we can do so only by understanding the "us" to which we belong, we would be wise to listen to Christians of previous generations on the issue of the sacraments.

It may not seem that the sacraments—especially as expounded by Christians of generations past—have much to teach us today about Christian identity, but that assumption says more about us moderns than it does about the sacraments themselves. One reason many of us fail to see the legitimacy of using the sacraments for answering questions pertaining to identity is that we do not understand just how profoundly both our personal and collective practices shape us and reveal who we are and what is most important to us.[1] Another reason is that we have been conditioned, to some degree, by the pragmatism of modern secular culture, which is preoccupied with the plights of humanity, political issues, personal needs, and countless other problems that need to be solved, and many of us have adopted an anthropological outlook on life, presupposing that the issues we face can be addressed by programs and organizations—whether political, religious, or otherwise—and nowadays especially by technology.[2] This mindset has affected the way we think about the ontology and mission of the church, corporate worship, and personal piety to such an extent that many of us inherently think that religion is primarily about us: what we can get out of it or how we can have enriching experiences in life. Thus, many of us innately suppose that the sacraments are

---

1   On the power of habits for identity and spiritual formation, see Dru Johnson, *Human Rites: The Power of Rituals, Habits, and Sacraments* (Grand Rapids, MI: Eerdmans, 2019).

2   See James B. Torrance, *Worship, Community and the Triune God of Grace* (Downers Grove, IL: InterVarsity Press, 1996), 70.

primarily human acts—and, ironically, acts that have little to no power to shape us.

We should in no way dismiss or trivialize human agency in observing the sacraments—after all, Christ has commanded *us* to be baptized and to eat and drink in remembrance of him, and he has ordained them for *our* use. Yet many of us today need to return to or more firmly embrace the truth handed down by the historic church that the sacraments are principally divine gifts. The sacraments are, as we have already touched on, means of grace as well as visible words of the gospel through which God communicates his goodness in Christ to his people by his Spirit. Baptism and Communion enable us to experience the gospel in a multisensory manner and so strengthen our faith in and even bond with Christ, the main subject matter of the sacraments. Only when we come to understand the sacraments as expounded by the historic church— the *us* to which we as individual members belong—are we able to properly grasp what they teach us about being in-Christ persons and therefore what they mean for personal identity, meaning, and purpose.[3]

Divine Witnesses

One primary feature of the sacraments that is emphasized by numerous Protestant confessions and catechisms is that they are aids

---

3 I am under no illusion that Christians throughout history have held a monolithic understanding of the sacraments. The sacraments are an issue on which many Christians have disagreed, often vehemently so. This is true even among Protestants. Yet there is a general consensus that I wish to uphold. My attempt in this chapter is to highlight what Protestants have broadly agreed on. For instance, the most premier Protestant confessions affirm that the sacraments are pledges or signs, even though these features are understood variously. When it comes to particular matters, I embrace a more Reformed perspective, which I believe makes the most sense biblically and theologically.

to faith. Scripture serves primarily to create faith in Christ, and it then strengthens faith by leading us to a deeper knowledge and experience of our triune God. The sacraments also strengthen and confirm our faith in him but do so by presenting Christ and his benefits to us in tangible form. Just as water hydrates, bread nourishes, and wine invigorates the body, so baptism and Communion fortify faith.

Already we can see the implications this sacramental function has for personal identity: it emphasizes that we are weak and limited, utterly dependent on God. As Christians, we know this is true not simply because we are sinners—and continue to be so even after we have been redeemed—but also because we are creatures, utterly contingent, dependent on and conditioned by something (or more accurately, *someone*) else. Like every other finite being, our existence is derivative; we derive it proximally from our parents yet ultimately from God, the one in whom we live and move and have our being (Acts 17:28). While it may not seem obvious, the sacraments reinforce these truths. They affirm that God is the source of all life and that he alone has the power to create, re-create, and sustain. We are not independent, self-sufficient beings but completely dependent and in need of continuous sustaining.

The reason the sacraments have such energizing power is that they are "sure witnesses . . . of grace, and God's good will towards us," as the Thirty-Nine Articles of Religion puts it.[4] Similarly, the Belgic Confession states that they "pledge [God's] good will and grace toward us."[5] For many Christians, especially evangelicals not formed by any particular confession, it is natural to think of the sacraments as "witnesses" or "pledges," though primarily as

4 Thirty-Nine Articles, art. 25 (*CCC* 125).
5 Belgic Confession, art. 33 (*CCC* 105).

witnesses or pledges of personal faith. Baptism and Communion are considered nothing more than performative rituals whereby we express our faith in Christ and commemorate his saving work.[6] To be sure, both Scripture and history confirm that the sacraments are expressions of personal faith as well as commemorative acts. In my own tradition, for example, the minister declares when leading the congregation to the Table of Holy Communion, "We celebrate the memorial of our redemption,"[7] and all the people remember, with cheerfulness and humble gratitude, what Christ has done for them. This language of commemoration is inspired by the words of Christ himself: "Do this in remembrance of me" (Luke 22:19). And the fact that Communion is an act of remembrance is reinforced by the reality that it is analogous to the Passover meal, which was itself a "memorial day" (Ex. 12:14) for Israelite families to gratefully ponder how the Lord God had delivered them from bondage in Egypt. Just as the people of Israel were to recall what the Lord had done for them when celebrating the Passover year after year, so we who have been made members of Christ's body are to recall what he has done for us as often as we eat the Supper. The sacrament of Communion is therefore a perpetual reminder for us that Christ is Lord and Savior, the one who has redeemed us by his broken body

6 Though I say that this understanding is held by many evangelicals today who are not formed by any particular confessional tradition, it does have precedent in history. Huldrych Zwingli, for one, argued that a sacrament is "nothing else than an initiatory ceremony or a pledging" by which people prove publicly to the church that they belong to Christ. Zwingli, *Commentary on True and False Religion*, ed. Samuel Macauley Jackson and Clarence Nevin Heller (1929; repr., Durham, NC: Labyrinth, 1981), 181. This view, however, does not make total sense of Scripture or the world in which it was written. Moreover, Zwingli's view represents a minority stance during the Reformation, which was countered by other major Reformers such as Martin Luther, John Calvin, Thomas Cranmer, and Peter Martyr Vermigli.

7 Anglican Church in North America, *The Book of Common Prayer* (Huntington Beach, CA: Anglican Liturgy Press, 2019), 133 (hereafter cited as *BCP*).

and shed blood—and that the same Lord will one day return to fully establish his kingdom on earth and feast with us in the flesh. The same could be said about baptism. Writing to the church in Rome, Paul asks, "Do you not know that all of us who have been baptized into Christ Jesus were baptized into his death?" (Rom. 6:3). Paul is not quizzing his audience but reminding them—and us as well—of what should be an obvious truth: baptism and union with Christ in his death and resurrection are tandem realities. For Paul, baptism points to something far greater than submersion into and emergence from water. Whatever else we might say about baptism, we can say at least this: it confronts us with Jesus Christ and the reality of what he has done for us, that he himself was baptized not only with the baptism of water in the Jordan but also with the baptism of death at Golgotha (Mark 10:38–39) so that we might die to sin and be raised to new life in him. So when we are baptized or witness another person being baptized, we recall and meditate on what Christ has done for us—at least this should be the natural response of the redeemed.

Baptism and Communion are events that lead us to meditate on Christ and his saving work. And as commemorative acts, they are also performative. By participating in the sacraments, we profess that we believe what we commemorate. By adhering to Christ's commands to be baptized and eat his meal, we demonstrate our faith before God and others.[8] To quote the Thirty-Nine Articles again, the sacraments are "badges or tokens of Christian men's profession."[9]

Yet when we consider Paul's words in Romans 6, we notice that baptism—and this is true for Communion also—is not simply

8   See Calvin, *Inst.*, 4.14.1, 13, 19.
9   Thirty-Nine Articles, art. 25 (*CCC* 125).

a commemorative act or an expression of personal faith. It is not primarily something *we* do. We are not the primary agents, and we are not the ones who give the act meaning or significance. Paul tells us we *were baptized*, using the passive voice, indicating that we were acted on from outside ourselves. Someone else was the primary agent, and we were the recipients of the activity. Baptism preaches the gospel, the good news of God's work *for us* and *to us* in Christ and by his Spirit. Thus, baptism points to a reality far greater than the act of being submerged in and raised from water. It signifies being crucified with Christ and being raised with him to new life, of our old self being drowned in a watery grave and our new self being raised to the surface of new creation. And it is that same new self that has been clothed with Christ himself (Gal. 3:27). We have been stripped of our old self and donned with a new one fashioned after the likeness of our glorious Redeemer— though we certainly continue to wrestle with the lingering power of sin and death in our lives. And the Supper of our Lord's passion is a "participation," a communion, in the body and the blood of Christ (1 Cor. 10:16), not just an act of remembrance. The sacraments, then, are far more than human activities whereby we ponder past events. They are, as the historic church has affirmed, divine gifts that point to a grand present reality and lead us to enjoy it more fully.

So when we confess that the sacraments are witnesses or pledges, we must refrain from adopting an anthropological approach, placing the human self at the center of attention and activity. The sacraments are not chiefly anthropological—a foundational point when considering the connection between the sacraments and identity. While the sacraments indeed speak to who we are, they do so only by way of teaching us who God is and what he has done. Thus, any anthropological significance they have is derived from their theological (in the strictest sense of the term—that is, a word about God) significance. The sacraments are ultimately about our triune God, what the Father has done through the Son by the power of the Holy Spirit. This means that the sacraments are not primarily witnesses or attestations of *our faith*. First and foremost, they are witnesses to *God's grace*, his promises set forth and accomplished in his Son and activated in our lives by the power of the Spirit.

This is why the term *sacrament* is richer and more theologically profound than *ordinance*, especially when we consider the significance that baptism and Communion have for personal identity. Language of *ordinance* emphasizes and often prioritizes human activity—*our* observing the rites that Christ instituted. Baptism and Communion are therefore seen primarily as human responses to what God has done for us in Christ.[10] While we are certainly commanded to be baptized and partake of Communion and to respond with faith and gratitude for what God has done for us, the language of *sacrament*, even though it is an extrabiblical term, rightly emphasizes the primacy of God's activity in these gospel gifts. The Latin word *sacramentum* was initially a military term, an oath by which a soldier bound himself in allegiance to his superiors. Eventually, Christians adopted the word and gave it a new meaning. As J. I. Packer explains, "The oath was understood to be God's, a promise guaranteeing salvation to everyone who receives Jesus Christ as Savior and Lord, professes penitent faith, and commits

---

10 That said, the language of *covenanting ordinances* comes much closer to what I believe baptism and Communion are. On the benefit of such language, which testifies to "the two-way street of pledged unity, fidelity, and tenacity—that is, love—that shapes the saving relationship between God the Father, the Son, and the Holy Spirit, and man the penitent believer," see J. I. Packer, *Taking God Seriously: Vital Things We Need to Know* (Wheaton, IL: Crossway, 2013), 132.

to be fully faithful to God throughout life."[11] Tertullian captures this new meaning while still alluding to the military oath when he states, "We are called to military service of the living God in our answer to the words of the sacrament (at baptism)."[12] While this human profession is vital in itself, Packer notes, it is "derivative, and thus of secondary importance compared to God's own pledge."[13] Thus John Calvin states, "By the sacraments the Lord promises that 'he will be our God and we shall be his people' [Jer. 30:22]."[14] The sacraments are primarily testimonies to God's grace toward us and secondarily attestations of our faith in and commitment to him.[15]

This emphasis has profound implications for personal identity. The world today tries to force-feed us the lie that we are our own and that we can generate our own meaning and purpose without external constraints from society or other individuals, but the sacraments teach us otherwise—and something immensely better. God has claimed us as his own and pledged himself to be our God. We are not autonomous beings who determine our own significance and can express it however we want but are redeemed creatures who derive our existence, meaning, and purpose from the Creator of all things. And it is this Creator who has stooped down in Christ to mark us as his own and has declared, "I will be your God, and you will be my people." He has not only pledged himself to us and made good on his promise to be favorable to us but also calls us to be faithful Christian soldiers, to live under his authority and command. In baptism and Communion, God promises that we

---

11 Packer, *Taking God Seriously*, 130.
12 Quoted in Geerhardus Vos, *Reformed Dogmatics: A System of Christian Theology*, single-vol. ed., trans. and ed. Richard B. Gaffin Jr. (Bellingham, WA: Lexham, 2020), 936.
13 Packer, *Taking God Seriously*, 130.
14 Calvin, *Inst.*, 4.14.13.
15 See Calvin, *Inst.*, 4.14.1.

may have new life, an entirely new existence, in his Son. So when we, with Spirit-created faith, encounter the water of baptism and the bread and wine of Communion, we should be reminded—and in a manner that affects our whole selves and not just our intellects—that we belong to the Lord of the universe, who alone is able to say, "All the earth is mine" (Ex. 19:5). And it is that same all-powerful God—who is also the God of all goodness, beauty, and truth—who has willed to be favorable and indulgent toward those united to his Son, whom he loves and with whom he is ever so pleased. Such knowledge melts all anxiety and fear, assuring us that we do not have to look inside ourselves or to the world for significance and purpose. We are loved and significant not because of our own personal narratives or achievements, which may or may not find approval in the eyes of the world, but because our triune God has made us his own.

Signs and Seals

In addition to seeing the sacraments as witnesses of divine favor, testimonies to what God has done in Christ for us and to who he wills to be in relation to us, we may describe them as "signs and seals of the covenant of grace," to use the language of the Westminster divines.[16] Here I do not care to distinguish sharply between the language of *witnesses* and *signs* since both terms are used to indicate that the sacraments testify to or are evidence of a reality greater than the witnesses or signs themselves. The phrase "signs and seals" is theologically potent, and numerous Protestant confessions—not to mention the many authors of individual theological works—have affirmed that baptism and Communion are

---

16 WCF 27.1 (*CCC* 227).

signs and seals of God's covenant grace.[17] Such writings adapt the phrase "signs and seals" from Paul's description of circumcision in Romans 4:11, where he explains that Abraham "received the sign of circumcision as a seal of the righteousness that he had by faith while he was still uncircumcised."[18] The application of the language in Romans 4 to baptism and Communion shows that they function in the administration of the new covenant in much the same way as circumcision and Passover did in the old.[19] But what does it mean that the sacraments are signs and seals? What do they signify or point to, and what do they seal or confirm—never mind in a manner that reveals something about Christian identity?

First, what exactly do the sacraments signify? A sign (Gk. *sēmeion*), as Paul uses the term in Romans 4:11, is a proof, an evidence, or a sure token.[20] The Augsburg Confession states that the sacraments are "signs and testimonies of the will of God toward us."[21] The Heidelberg Catechism declares that God instituted baptism and Communion so that we could "understand more clearly the promise of the gospel."[22] Or, returning to the Westminster Confession, the sacraments "represent Christ, and his benefits," and thereby "confirm our interest in him."[23] Heirs of the Refor-

---

17 See Augsburg Confession, art. 13 (*CCC* 40); Belgic Confession, art. 33 (*CCC* 105); Thirty-Nine Articles, art. 25 (*CCC* 125); WCF 27.1 (*CCC* 227); 1689 London Baptist Confession, 29.1 (*CCC* 284). While all these confessions use the language of *signs*, not all use the language of *seals*.

18 See Derek W. H. Thomas, "Covenant, Assurance, and the Sacraments," in *Covenant Theology: Biblical, Theological, and Historical Perspectives*, ed. Guy Prentiss Waters, J. Nicholas Reid, and John R. Muether (Wheaton, IL: Crossway, 2020), 572.

19 Thomas, "Covenant, Assurance, and the Sacraments," 572.

20 See William D. Mounce, ed., *Mounce's Complete Expository Dictionary of Old and New Testament Words* (Grand Rapids, MI: Zondervan, 2006), 1268.

21 Augsburg Confession, art. 13 (*CCC* 40).

22 Heidelberg Catechism, q. 66 (*CCC* 309).

23 WCF 27.1 (*CCC* 227).

mation have univocally affirmed that the sacraments declare the good news of God's love in Christ in visible, physical form. This is why, as we touched on in the previous chapter, baptism and Communion are visible words of the gospel. As Derek Thomas explains, "They portray fundamental blessings (and curses) of the gospel. They do so both in an exhibitive manner (by pointing in the direction of the sacrament's meaning and intent), and in a communicative manner (the sacraments are themselves a demonstration of gospel blessing)."[24] This means that the sacraments "are not empty and hollow signs to fool and deceive us, for their truth *is Jesus Christ*, without whom they would be nothing," as the Belgic Confession declares.[25] They are not mere images or rituals that simply depict ideas and events. To be sure, baptism and Communion are symbolic and *represent* theological realities, but they also *present* those realities to us in a way that makes them personal realities when they are received with faith. As Geerhardus Vos explains, "The sacraments are no *nuda signa*, 'bare signs,' no *signa theoretica*, 'theoretical signs.'" Rather, they are "*signa practica*, 'practical signs.' When they are used in faith, the user receives, by the working of the Holy Spirit, the grace that they portray and seal."[26] They are indeed *means* of grace, having an effectual quality in addition to a declarative quality. Vos further expounds,

> In the New Testament dispensation, there is really no place for symbols that are not means of grace, since the shadows have passed away and the body has come. The sacramental expressions

24 Thomas, "Covenant, Assurance, and the Sacraments," 572–73.

25 Belgic Confession, art. 33 (*CCC* 105; emphasis added).

26 Vos, *Reformed Dogmatics*, 940. Cf. Robert Bruce, *The Mystery of the Lord's Supper: Sermons on the Sacrament Preached in the Kirk of Edinburgh in A.D. 1589 by Robert Bruce*, trans. and ed. Thomas F. Torrance (London: James Clarke, 1958), 44.

of Scripture, which present the thing signified and the sign in such close conjunction, become completely inexplicable if one continues to adhere to the concept of symbol.[27]

The *signum* (the "sign") and the *res* (the "thing" signified) are so closely conjoined ultimately because of the incarnation. God has, in his Son, joined himself to humanity, joined the spiritual and the physical, and therefore does not operate by mere symbols but communicates himself through objects that he has chosen to be fitting instruments of his work. He does not act at a distance or in abstraction but rather in proximity and in a concrete manner. And while not depreciating the significance of the incarnation, we must understand that God has always worked in our world through physical means. He does not operate purely on a supernatural level. In fact, the very distinction between natural and supernatural can be problematic. To be sure, the apostle Paul distinguishes between what is "natural" and what is "spiritual" (1 Cor. 2:14–15). But this distinction is not between matter and spirit per se. It is between what is animated and influenced by the Holy Spirit and what is not.[28] The supposition of a natural-supernatural world in which God operates primarily by supernatural means apart from anything natural or physical reflects more of a modern mindset than a biblical one.[29]

---

27 Vos, *Reformed Dogmatics*, 988.

28 See Richard B. Gaffin Jr., *In the Fullness of Time: An Introduction to the Biblical Theology of Acts and Paul* (Wheaton, IL: Crossway, 2022), 326–27.

29 See Charles Taylor, *A Secular Age* (Cambridge, MA: Belknap Press of Harvard University Press, 2007), 542. Taylor argues that the natural-supernatural distinction—which "was originally made in order to mark the autonomy of the supernatural" and used by the Reformers "to disentangle the order of grace from that of nature"—was an achievement of the Middle Ages and early modern period that eventually, among other factors, led people way from an "enchanted" view of the world, a view in which spirits of various kinds are active in our

All this means that when baptism is received with faith, the recipient *actually* receives cleansing from sin, forgiveness of sin, new life, the indwelling of the Spirit, adoption, and incorporation into the church. And when Communion is received with faith, the recipient *actually* participates in the body and blood of Christ and thus receives his benefits of redemption, is nourished to greater faith, is sustained to everlasting life, and is joined more tightly to Christ and his body, the church. The sacraments are instruments through which God works to communicate his good grace to his children—both *conveying* it to them and *conferring* it on them—so long as Spirit-created faith in Christ is operative within us.

As signs of the gospel, the sacraments also function as microcosms of Christ's redemptive-historical work. At this point, we return to our earlier discussion of the sacraments as commemorative acts. The sacraments cause us to ponder Christ's redemptive-historical work because they point or lead us to Christ, his work, and his benefits. Baptism leads us to think on his identification with humanity, his messianic ministry, and his death and resurrection. Because of the work of the Son, we are adopted and made heirs with him, washed of our sins and given his purity, raised from death and given his life. Communion causes us to think on Christ's sacrifice, that his broken body and spilled blood have redeemed us and restored our communion with the Father, who reigns with the Son and Spirit forever, and our communion with one another.

---

world. Granted, not all understandings of an "enchanted" world are biblical, but they do recognize the inextricability of the natural and supernatural. What is problematic about the version of the natural-supernatural distinction that many modern Christians embrace is not so much the affirmation of the superiority of grace but the supposition that God works apart from physical means. This notion not only offends the incarnation but also neglects the fact that it is impossible for humans to experience God apart from such means because we are physical-spiritual creatures who experience God *in our bodies*.

When we encounter baptism and Communion, we therefore are immersed into the gospel story itself, a story that has been made ours because we are united to Christ.

When I say that the gospel story has been made ours, I do not mean that we participate in accomplishing redemption. Rather, I mean that we have been invited into the Christ story to the extent that his story of humiliation, death, and resurrection is now ours by virtue of our union with him. The gospel is not just an account of extraordinary events that occurred long ago—though it certainly is the good news of what the historical Christ has done once and for all. It is also our narrative and thus is determinative for our lives, our identities, our very selves.

The question is, How well do we live according to the gospel story? "Everyone lives and operates out of some narrative identity," explains Timothy Keller, "whether it is thought out and reflected upon or not."[30] And so, as Alister McGrath puts it, "The story we believe we are in determines what we think about ourselves and consequently how we live."[31] Commenting on the current landscape, McGrath identifies the stories of progress and victimhood as the two main stories forming identity today:

Some live under the story of individual progress of the sort peddled on daytime talk shows, that the self is the most important

30 Timothy Keller, *The Reason for God: Belief in an Age of Skepticism* (New York: Dutton, 2008), 15. I became aware of this Keller quote along with the following Alister McGrath quotes in my reading of Brian Rosner, *How to Find Yourself: Why Looking Inward Is Not the Answer* (Wheaton, IL: Crossway, 2022). Rosner's book is a helpful study on identity, and in working through his book, I became aware of multiple sources to consult and quote from.

31 Alister McGrath, *Deep Magic, Dragons and Talking Mice: How Reading C. S. Lewis Can Change Your Life* (London: Hodder and Stoughton, 2014), 47, quoted in Rosner, *How to Find Yourself*, 117.

thing there is and that more or better information will organically produce better selves. Still others subscribe to the victim metanarrative, that their personal choices have little impact on the world they live in.[32]

Brian Rosner identifies the stories of secular materialism and social justice as the two big stories most profoundly shaping people in the West today.[33] The sacraments teach us that we do not live according to the narrative of those who belong to the world but to the story of our crucified and risen Lord, and as we participate in the sacraments, we actually participate in the gospel story. As Tim Chester explains,

> Our baptism brings those past events [Christ's death and resurrection] *into our present.* We physically reenact the drama of the story. United with Christ, we are "buried" under the water (through whatever mode of baptism is used), before rising again out of the water to a new life—a point Paul makes in Romans 6:3–4. We reenact the story in baptism not just to remember it but also to make it our own. Communion, too, brings the past event of Christ's death into the present. We remember, but by remembering we make the benefits of his death our own. The past becomes a present reality, and we are assured of the forgiveness of our sins.[34]

While the sacraments are not the whole of the Christian life— meaning that the Christian life, in both its personal and corporate

---

32 McGrath, *Deep Magic, Dragons and Talking Mice*, 70, quoted in Rosner, *How to Find Yourself,* 120n12.

33 Rosner, *How to Find Yourself,* 120.

34 Tim Chester, *Truth We Can Touch: How Baptism and Communion Shape Our Lives* (Wheaton, IL: Crossway, 2020), 113; emphasis added.

expressions, cannot be reduced to the celebration of baptism and Communion—they are *symbolic of the whole Christian life*, signifying the essence of life in Christ because they preach Christ, who is our life (Col. 3:4), and his life story. As Louis-Marie Chauvet explains, a symbol *"crystallizes"* the world to which it points, in such a way that it represents "the whole of the world to which it belongs."[35] As signs of the gospel, of Christ and his benefits, the sacraments point to the world of the gospel and what it means to live life as citizens of that world. Or they are, to use W. H. Griffith Thomas's phrase, "expressions in act of what the Gospel is intended to be."[36]

As baptized persons, immersed into Christ and his story, who commune with the triune God and his people, we do not live according to the stories of those belonging to the world, which ebb and flow with the tides of culture. We are not isolated selves who live under the story of individual progress, in which who we are and what we become—usually determined by our own particular tastes or preferences—are most important. We are not determined ultimately by any injustice committed against us, and we certainly are not defined primarily by whatever social and political causes we stand for.[37] We are not merely physical beings, people who can

35 Louis-Marie Chauvet, *The Sacraments: The Word of God at the Mercy of the Body*, trans. Madeleine Beaumont (Collegeville, MN: Liturgical Press, 2001), 71–72; emphasis original.

36 W. H. Griffith Thomas, *The Principles of Theology: An Introduction to the Thirty-Nine Articles* (London: Longmans, Green, 1930), 344. Packer similarly explains that baptism and Communion signify, symbolize, and seal "the essence of true Christianity"—"union and communion" with Christ. Packer, *Taking God Seriously*, 128.

37 The topic of social justice is much debated nowadays, and I do not wish to dismiss justice outright. Justice is a significant theme in Scripture, and Christians are called to promote and maintain what is right, especially on behalf of legitimate victims, at the societal level. God is just, and he calls his children to walk according to his justice. The problem with various strands of the social-justice narrative today is that their concepts of justice do not align with biblical justice—they want justice without judgment—and the practices of many

advance in life simply by working hard enough and using our intellects well, people who are characterized and ultimately fulfilled
by the possessions we obtain, people who can live life and express
ourselves—and thus use our bodies—however we want because
there is no divine reality or law. To live according to the stories of
the world—the ways of sinful people alienated from God—leads
only to destruction and despair.

We are children of God and belong to a holy family. We thus
live not according to the flesh but according to the Spirit of God,
who brings life and peace. We are more than conquerors, and no
one and nothing is able to separate us from the God of glory or the
benefits he offers us in his Son. We are people who live generously
and sacrificially because the God to whom we have been reconciled
is a generous and self-giving God. These truths are crystallized in
baptism and Communion, which declare that we are in Christ
and Christ is in us.

As profound as it is that the sacraments are signs of the gospel
that point us to Christ and his benefits, they are more than signs.
They not only *portray* but also *confirm* gospel realities, and so they
are *seals* as well. A seal (Gk. *sphragis*) is a mark of authority and
validation. Just as a stamp on a letter confirms the document, so
the sacraments confirm the realities they portray. This means that
what is sealed is not our faith but "the gospel itself in its multi-
dimensional nature of regeneration, new creation, justification,
and glorification."[38] Or as Calvin explains, the sacraments seal or
imprint "the promises of God . . . on our hearts" and thus confirm

---

who seek justice do not necessarily align with the practices that God calls us to adopt. For a
helpful discussion of the social-justice narrative and its shortcomings, especially in relation
to personal identity, see Rosner, *How to Find Yourself*, 143–61.

38 Thomas, "Covenant, Assurance, and the Sacraments," 574.

"the certainty of grace."[39] We humans are fragile, and even our faith is imperfect and weak, but the grace of God is sure. What he has declared to be true—that by faith we may have an entirely new existence in his Son—is confirmed by baptism and Communion. All of us yearn for security and meaning and purpose, and if we look to ourselves, other sinful humans, or our circumstances for these, despair will inevitably overtake us. The sacraments teach us to look outside ourselves, our changing circumstances, and the broken world around us to the Lord alone for the longings of our hearts. They not only present to us a Savior who is favorable but also confirm in our hearts and minds that he is indeed so *to us*.

A seal also functions as a mark of possession and identity.[40] Early Christians compared the sacraments, baptism in particular, to "a brand on an animal, a mark on a slave, or a regimental tattoo on a Roman solider."[41] As divine seals, baptism and Communion mark us as God's special possession. In my own tradition, for example, the minster says to the newly baptized person, "You are sealed by the Holy Spirit in Baptism and marked as Christ's own for ever."[42] To borrow the maxim that Calvin uses to capture the essence of the Christian life, *Nostri non sumus, sed Domini* (We are not our own, but the Lord's).[43] We are set apart as members

39 John Calvin, *The Epistles of Paul the Apostle to the Romans and to the Thessalonians*, ed. David W. Torrance and Thomas F. Torrance, trans. Ross Mackenzie, CNTC 8 (1960; repr., Grand Rapids, MI: Eerdmans, 1980), 89 (on Rom. 4:11). See also *Inst.*, 4.14.1, where Calvin describes the sacraments as outward signs "by which the Lord seals on our consciences the promises of his good will toward us in order to sustain the weakness of our faith."
40 See Peter J. Leithart, *Baptism: A Guide to Life from Death* (Bellingham, WA: Lexham, 2021), 16. I am indebted to Leithart for much of the content in this paragraph.
41 See Leithart, *Baptism*, 16; Jean Daniélou, *The Bible and the Liturgy* (Notre Dame, IN: University of Notre Dame Press, 1956), 58–59.
42 *BCP* 169, 189.
43 Calvin, *Inst.*, 3.7.1.

of God's flock, servants in his house, and soldiers under his command. Who we are, therefore, is ultimately determined not by what we do or accomplish or by who we wish to be but by the one who has claimed us as his own, the God of the gospel. Consequently, we are expected to live and behave in a manner that honors the name of our triune God, the name with which we are sealed. In the sacraments, we receive not only the promises and benefits of the gospel but also its demands, which subvert worldly notions of the self—its nature, purpose, and capabilities. As sheep, we follow our great shepherd. As slaves, we obey and serve our master. As soldiers, we follow the orders of and fight for our great commander. And this is no abhorrent task. The one to whom we belong is good and loving, and he has our best interests always in view. As Peter Leithart explains, "Good shepherds care for their sheep. Good masters love their slaves. Good generals provide for their troops."[44]

Formative Rituals

The fact that the sacraments are signs and seals through which God testifies his grace to us and confirms it in our hearts and minds does not negate the fact that they are also rituals that we perform. As the Thirty-Nine Articles declares, "The Sacraments were not ordained of Christ to be gazed upon, or to be carried about, but that *we should duly use them.*"[45] They were instituted by Christ for our use and benefit. We are indeed performative agents when we participate in the sacraments because thereby we express and embody our identification with Christ and his body. And because such performative action is underpinned by faith in Christ and

44 Leithart, *Baptism*, 16–17.
45 Thirty-Nine Articles, art. 25 (*CCC* 125; emphasis added).

internal transformation by his Spirit, it is also formative, shaping us more into Christlike persons.

What we do influences who we are. Our habits form the way we think, feel, and act. This truth does not trivialize the power of knowledge for shaping who we are. Of all people, Christians know the power of knowledge because we serve and worship Jesus Christ, the eternal Logos (John 1:1), who alone is "the way and *the truth* and the life" (John 14:6). He alone has "the words of eternal life" (John 6:68). He is the logic of creation, the one who makes sense of all that exists, because by him and through him all things were made and hold together, and he is reconciling all things to himself (Col. 1:16–17, 20). And as we study and embrace the truth about him, the living Word of God, in Scripture, the written word of God, we are transformed into his likeness. The apostle Paul affirms this when he tells the church in Rome that we as Christ followers are transformed when our minds are renewed (Rom. 12:2). And Christ himself declares that we are sanctified by the truth (John 17:19).

Yet if we are shaped only by knowledge, Paul—and so many others throughout Scripture—would not have been so outspoken about actions, cautioning us against sinful behavior and exhorting us to godly conduct. Consider Paul's warning against sexual immorality in 1 Corinthians 6, where he suggests that our behavior both stems from and shapes our identity. He writes, "Do you not know that your bodies are members of Christ? Shall I then take the members of Christ and make them members of a prostitute? Never! Or do you not know that he who is joined to a prostitute becomes one body with her?" (1 Cor. 6:15–16). Paul's point is that our conduct is driven by who we are and understand ourselves to be. If we are in Christ, then we ought to act—using all our body parts and not just our minds—as though we belong to him and are indeed one with him. Yet our actions also shape who we become—and in the particular situation that Paul addresses here, frighteningly so. A man who joins himself to a woman not his wife becomes united with her; he becomes one flesh with her. His very self and not just his body is now somehow entangled with her self. His behavior, therefore, is not simply physical with no relational or spiritual consequences but rather profoundly formative—or rather in this case, *deformative*. His very self is altered the moment he gives himself to her.

My intention here is not to highlight the seriousness of sexual sin but to stress the power of our actions and habits. As C. S. Lewis observes,

> Every time you make a choice you are turning the central part of you, the part of you that chooses, *into something a little different* from what it was before. And taking your life as a whole, with all your innumerable choices, all your life long you are slowly turning this central thing into a heavenly creature or a hellish creature.[46]

Negatively, our sinful choices and behaviors, which spring from the lingering power of sin in our lives, conform us to the pattern of this world, making us "hellish." Positively, our godly choices and behaviors, which are inspired and empowered by the Holy Spirit, conform us more to the image of Christ, making us "heavenly." Everything we do has some effect on who we are.[47]

---

46 C. S. Lewis, *Mere Christianity* (1952; repr., New York: Touchstone, 1996), 87; emphasis added.

47 See Rosner, *How to Find Yourself*, 49–50.

Because our actions and indeed our rhythms of life are so profoundly consequential, our participation in the sacraments plays a vital role in our Christian formation. The sacraments certainly help us understand more richly what Christ has done and who we are in him. Yet they also possess potency to make us more like him. As means of grace, they give us the life-altering benefits that they portray, so long as Spirit-created faith is operative within us.

The sacraments also contribute significantly to our self-understanding, though in a way that does not promote self-obsession or self-actualization. At this point, it is helpful to return to the commemorative nature of participating in the sacraments and consider the power of remembrance. As Grant Macaskill writes, "Our identities are very closely linked to our memories. *Who we are* is shaped by *what we remember* because our identity is, in part at least, narrative, and our memories constitute our story."[48] When we remember our past, we think about the people and events that have contributed to our own personal formation. Dementia is a prime yet frightening example of this truth "because those whose memories are compromised appear to be losing themselves or to be lost to those around them."[49] The power to remember shapes our perception of ourselves, which shapes the way we carry ourselves, present ourselves to others, and interact with others, all of which in turn shapes the ways that others perceive us and relate to us. It is impossible, therefore, not to be shaped by others and their stories. Christian or otherwise, we all belong to some group, and we all are formed by countless other people. Our particular narratives are shaped by the narratives of others.

48 Grant Macaskill, *Living in Union with Christ: Paul's Gospel and Christian Moral Identity* (Grand Rapids, MI: Baker Academic, 2019), 73; emphasis original.
49 Macaskill, *Living in Union with Christ*, 75–76.

So when we recall the Christ story while celebrating the sacraments, we are not simply pondering the past events of some person unrelated to us. We are remembering the story of a person to whom we are inextricably united by Spirit-created faith, and such acts of holy commemoration actually form who we are because the Christ story shapes our own stories. So when we think on our own baptism and partake of Communion, we remember not just who Christ is and what he has done for us but also who we are and are called to be in him. In these holy acts, we are reminded that we are baptized persons who commune with the triune God and his children, and such knowledge shapes the way we live.[50]

And since the sacraments are not just commemorative acts but also signs—visible words—of the gospel, they help us behold the truth continually. We are visual beings, and what we gaze on shapes profoundly who we are and what we do.[51] As our Lord said,

Your eye is the lamp of your body. When your eye is healthy, your whole body is full of light, but when it is bad, your body is full of darkness. Therefore be careful lest the light in you be darkness. If then your whole body is full of light, having no part

---

50 Johnson correctly states, "Memorials in Scripture are . . . about the communal classroom that shapes a people's knowledge of itself and the world over time." Johnson, *Human Rites*, 99.

51 I do not intend to dismiss or overlook blind people. Certainly, their lack of sight means their formation experiences are different (though not entirely) from those who can see, but that does not mean they are less human. All humans experience the effects of the fall, and blind people experience those effects in a particular way. Blind people who are in Christ, however, will one day receive a resurrected body that will behold the risen Lord and so be transformed by that sight, for "when he appears we shall be like him, because we shall see him as he is" (1 John 3:2). Though not everyone can set their physical eyes on objects, everyone can set the eyes of their hearts, their affections, on objects. So while the connection between physical sight and affection, and thus transformation, is indeed profound, what I hope is most clear in this section is the power of beholding in a spiritual manner, setting the gaze of our hearts on something or someone.

dark, it will be wholly bright, as when a lamp with its rays gives you light. (Luke 11:34–36)

No doubt, Christ is talking about spiritual sight—faith. Do we have faith in him? Are we illuminated to see the truth of who he is, and in such a way that our whole selves are made well? Before we are illuminated and led to faith by the Spirit, we are not able to see Christ clearly or walk without stumbling. Yet once the light of Christ opens the eyes of our hearts, we are able to see him for who he is, and our whole beings are made healthy. Yet his teaching here reinforces the power of sight—of setting our eyes and therefore our thoughts and affections on a certain object—and how it shapes our whole existence. We were created to behold and gaze on something. The question is, What are we gazing on, and does that object embody truth and lead to satisfaction?

We live in an image-driven world where images of countless varieties vie for our attention, affection, and allegiance. And whether or not we realize it, many of us are looking to these for personal meaning, purpose, and gratification, but what we fixate on usually leaves us wanting. For example, many young people, especially teen girls, are spending hours a day on social media but are becoming only lonelier and more depressed.[52] Countless people, including many Christians, are gazing continually on images that promote lies, twist reality, or present a false notion of self and thus are sinking into despair. We need the light of Christ to illuminate us daily to understand reality, even ourselves, correctly.

One way to continually gaze on Christ, the light of the world who helps us see all things clearly, is by participating regularly in

52 Jonathan Haidt, "Social Media Is a Major Cause of the Mental Illness Epidemic in Teen Girls. Here's the Evidence," *After Babel* (blog), February 22, 2023, https://jonathanhaidt.substack.com/.

the sacraments.[53] Whenever these visible words of the gospel are celebrated in the context of the gathered body, the crucified and risen Lord invites us to gaze on him and picture with sanctified imaginations the world to which we belong, the world of the gospel. When we accept his invitation and look with eyes of faith, we cannot help but become more enamored, and thus transformed, by what we behold—not the water, bread, and wine themselves but the reality to which they point, Christ and his benefits. Baptism and Communion help us become more captivated by Christ and his narrative. And the more we are immersed into his story, the more we are shaped by it. As Jonathan Gottschall explains, story "is one of the primary sculpting forces of individuals and societies." Indeed, he adds, "Stories are working on us all the time, reshaping us in the way that flowing water gradually shapes a rock."[54] The sacraments immerse us into and fill us with the story of Christ and allow it to continually work on us. They enable us to behold the glory of our crucified and risen Lord. And as we behold his glory, we are "transformed into the same image from one degree of glory to another" (2 Cor. 3:18).

It is for these reasons that we would be wise, I believe, to embrace a sacramental piety.[55] By *sacramental piety*, I mean a manner of life

---

53 This statement may seem to contradict art. 25 of the Thirty-Nine Articles, which states, "The Sacraments were not ordained of Christ to be gazed upon." This, however, is a reference to abuses common during the medieval and Reformation eras, such as undue veneration of the sacraments and confusion of the thing signified with the sign itself.

54 Jonathan Gottschall, *The Storytelling Animal: How Stories Make Us Human* (Boston: Mariner Books, 2013), 153.

55 I am expanding Wolfhart Pannenberg's prescription of a "eucharistic piety" to inoculate evangelicals against individualism. Wolfhart Pannenberg, *Christian Spirituality* (Philadelphia: Westminster, 1983), 31–49. See also Joel Scandrett, "Reclaiming Eucharistic Piety: A Postmodern Possibility for American Evangelicals?," in *Ancient and Postmodern Christianity: Paleo-Orthodoxy in the 21st Century; Essays in Honor of Thomas C. Oden*, ed. Kenneth Tanner and Christopher A. Hall (Downers Grove, IL: InterVarsity Press, 2002), 155–69.

that takes hold of the gifts of God and is consciously grounded in and oriented toward the sacraments—necessarily integrated with continuous feeding on Scripture, of course. No doubt, this means more regular participation in the sacraments, for we benefit greatly by participating in them more frequently, just as we benefit by engaging the word of God more frequently. Yet, more importantly, such a piety requires that we understand more deeply, *and thus embrace and enact*, what baptism and Communion portray and confirm. Put differently, a sacramental piety is a way of life that holds fast to the gifts God has given his church and that springs from a robust understanding of what it means to be baptized persons who commune with the triune God and his children.

As followers of Christ, we benefit from the water and blood that flowed from his side (John 19:34), and the sacraments of baptism and Communion portray those truths to us and invite us to participate in them. And when we embrace the sacraments with faith, they strengthen our identity as in-Christ persons. With that remarkable truth in mind, let us now turn our attention to what it means to be baptized and communing persons, to be persons of the water and the blood, and how that identity gives meaning to and shapes who we are as particular persons.

3

Baptized Persons

TO DESCRIBE OURSELVES TO OTHERS, and indeed understand ourselves, we use labels. This is unavoidable because we need to work with concepts in order to communicate to others something of who we are. And thus many of us use categories from personality tests and models of the psyche that promise to pinpoint our distinct makeup and temperament. Or we use labels that describe our current life stage, occupation, and affiliations. Some of us use political labels or even categories describing our sexuality. In doing so, we suppose that such labels and categories reveal the essence of who we.

Too often, however, we do not realize just how powerful labels are. The labels we use for ourselves not only reveal who we perceive ourselves to be but also shape how we live. One example of this is personality profiling. A person believes, or has been told, that he or she has a certain personality, and that person then acts in ways that correspond to that supposed personality. In our modern world, we have seemingly endless options for how to categorize and present ourselves, and a serious problem occurs when the labels we apply to ourselves are inadequate or inappropriate.[1] Sadly, many of us Christians today use nonbiblical categories when thinking about ourselves and our identity—or we use fitting categories in a disordered manner, giving them priority over other labels that should take precedence. Thankfully, we have guides from both Scripture and history to help us reevaluate and reorder the labels we are using to define ourselves and embrace others that accurately reflect who we are and are called to be as in-Christ persons.

Consider how Martin Luther describes himself: "I am a son of God, I am baptized, I believe in Jesus Christ crucified for me."[2] And ponder his advice for dealing with spiritual vexation: "The only way to drive away the Devil is through faith in Christ, by saying: 'I have been baptized, I am a Christian.'"[3] Luther describes himself as a Christian, yes, but also as a baptized person, as though it were impossible to be one without also being the other.

Using *baptized* as a primary label to describe oneself is uncommon for many Christians today. Perhaps this is because baptism is often considered a one-off experience with little to no lasting significance rather than a life-altering event that determines our very existence. This is the case because many Christians, especially those not formed by a particular confessional heritage, tend to have a minimalistic view of baptism and what it signifies and seals. They have also witnessed others who were once baptized, either at infancy or in adulthood, now living godless lives as hypocrites or apostates.

---

1 See Carl R. Trueman, *The Rise and Triumph of the Modern Self: Cultural Amnesia, Expressive Individualism, and the Road to Sexual Revolution* (Wheaton, IL: Crossway, 2020), 390–91.

2 Martin Luther, *D. Martin Luthers Werke, Kritische Gesamtausgabe: Tischreden* (Weimar: Böhlaus, 2000), 5:295. Translation by Wes Bredenhoff, "Luther: *Baptizatus sum* (I Am Baptized)," *Bredenhoff* (blog), January 26, 2017, https://bredenhof.ca/; translation slightly altered.

3 Quoted in Heiko Oberman, *Luther: Man between God and the Devil*, trans. Eileen Walliser-Schwarzbart (1989; repr., New Haven, CT: Yale University Press, 2006), 105.

In the latter scenario, baptism clearly has had no bearing on personal identity and morality. But this lamentable situation does not nullify the biblical truth that baptism and faith are meant to be tandem realities and that when the former is embraced with the latter, it is a powerful event and symbol—one that not only brings about a new existence but also shapes our self-consciousness. The sacrament of water is an instrument through which God works to signify and seal his covenant promises, and it governs the Christian's entire existence by portraying who the Christian is and is called to be in Christ.

It is for this reason that Luther can say, "A Christian life is nothing else than a daily baptism."[4] This much has been affirmed by countless other Christians throughout history because baptism is a template for Christian living. Moreover, baptism is "the initiatory rite of Christian identity," as Grant Macaskill puts it.[5] If we are to understand what it means to be a Christian and what it means to have our identity located in and defined by Christ, what it means to be in him and what bearing our union with him has on our existence as particular persons, we must recapture the language and meaning of being "baptized" and what that category means for personal identity. Yet we also need to embrace a biblical concept of baptism, which will no doubt challenge us to reassess the most fundamental aspects of who we are. In this chapter, therefore, we explore what it means to be a baptized person—to be a person who, with faith, embraces and embodies what baptism signifies and seals.

4 Martin Luther, "The Large Catechism," in *The Book of Concord: The Confessions of the Evangelical Lutheran Church*, ed. Robert Kolb and Timothy J. Wengert, trans. Charles Arand et al. (Minneapolis: Fortress, 2000), 465.

5 Grant Macaskill, *Living in Union with Christ: Paul's Gospel and Christian Moral Identity* (Grand Rapids, MI: Baker Academic, 2019), 59.

A New Identity

Baptism is a rite, a practice, an event that is concerned with identity.[6] *Baptism* transliterates the Greek noun *baptisma*, which means "immersion," and the verb *baptizō* literally means "to put or go under water," though it carries several other senses.[7] William Mounce shows that in the New Testament, *baptizō* is used to describe ceremonial washing, especially that which was practiced in the Israelite tradition for the purpose of purification. It is also used "to describe the use of water in a rite for the purpose of establishing or renewing a relationship with God," and so it "became a technical term."[8] Throughout the New Testament, we read of persons being baptized when they come to faith in Jesus Christ, signifying that they have entered into a covenant relationship with the triune God.[9] Baptism was not considered optional, left to the conscience of the individual once he or she felt ready or when the church felt the person was ready.[10] And the verb—when applied to those receiving the rite—is always used in the passive or middle voice, never in the active, meaning that "baptism is thus fundamentally and primarily *something from God to us*, not from us to God."[11] God is the one who establishes a new relationship with us. Yet the New Testament speaks not just of persons being baptized with water. It speaks of persons being

6 See Peter J. Leithart, *The Baptized Body* (Moscow, ID: Canon, 2007), 4–7.

7 William D. Mounce, ed., *Mounce's Complete Expository Dictionary of Old and New Testament Words* (Grand Rapids, MI: Zondervan, 2006), 52.

8 Mounce, *Complete Expository Dictionary*, 53.

9 See John Murray, *Christian Baptism* (Nutley, NJ: Presbyterian and Reformed, 1977), 6–7.

10 Anthony Lane, "Dual-Practice Baptism View," in *Baptism: Three Views*, ed. David F. Wright, Spectrum Multiview Books (Downers Grove, IL: IVP Academic, 2009), 143.

11 W. H. Griffith Thomas, *The Principles of Theology: An Introduction to the Thirty-Nine Articles* (London: Longmans, Green, 1930), 372; emphasis added.

baptized *into Christ* (Rom. 6:3–4; Gal. 3:26–27).[12] The sacrament
of baptism therefore signifies and seals the reality of being immersed into Christ, of being united with him and plunged into
a new existence in relation to him. In short, baptism exhibits
union with Christ.[13]

It is vital to understand that our union with Christ, our immersion into him, is possible because he first immersed himself
into us and united himself with us in our humanity. This is the
effect of his incarnation, taking on our human nature, as well as
of his own baptism—not just into the waters of the Jordan but
also into death at Golgotha.[14] John Clark and Marcus Johnson
explain,

> Jesus's baptism at the Jordan is the sign and seal of his im-
> mersion into the reality of identification with sin and sinners,
> of his entry into the state of human existence east of Eden to
> assume what is ours and make it his own. . . . Jesus's baptism
> at Golgotha is the sign and seal of his immersion into the real-
> ity of divine judgment, of his bringing to completion God's

12 See Mounce, *Complete Expository Dictionary*, 53. Geerhardus Vos similarly states that baptism brings persons into personal relationship with the triune God. Vos, *Reformed Dogmatics: A System of Christian Theology*, single-vol. ed., trans. and ed. Richard B. Gaffin Jr. (Bellingham, WA: Lexham, 2020), 977–78.

13 See J. I. Packer, *Concise Theology* (Wheaton, IL: Crossway, 2020), 223–26; Murray, *Christian Baptism*, 6, 8, 34.

14 In fact, Jesus's baptism into the waters of the Jordan anticipates his baptism into death at Golgotha. The Synoptic Gospels report that when Jesus came up from the water, a voice from heaven declared, "You are my beloved Son" (Mark. 1:11; Luke 3:22; cf. Matt. 3:17), which is likely a reference to Ps. 2:7, and the Holy Spirit descended on him (Matt. 3:16; Mark. 1:10; Luke 3:22), which is perhaps a reference to the Lord's servant in Isa. 42:1 ("I have put my Spirit upon him"), the same servant who was to suffer for his people (Isa. 52:13–53:12). Christ's baptism in the Jordan is therefore his inauguration as *the Messiah come to die*. See Everett Ferguson, *Baptism in the Early Church: History, Theology, and Liturgy in the First Five Centuries* (Grand Rapids, MI: Eerdmans, 2009), 101.

condemnation of sin in the flesh he assumed for us and our salvation.[15]

The Son of God became one of us and identified himself with us so that we might become one with him and identify with him, to receive his benefits and become like him.

It is no surprise, then, that the first Christians were baptized *in the name of the Lord Jesus* (Acts 2:38; 8:16; 10:48; 19:5) because he is the Messiah in whom we find salvation, and union with him is, as J. I. Packer explains, "the source of every element in our salvation (1 John 5:11–12)."[16] The phrase *in the name of Jesus* is likely shorthand for the Trinitarian formula outlined in Matthew 28:19 since it is through the Son that we have access to the Father and receive the Holy Spirit.[17] To be baptized in Jesus's name certainly means to be brought under his ownership and lordship, and that fact should not be underappreciated.[18] But it means even more than that. "Names are, after all, core elements in identity," Macaskill observes. Language of *in the name of Jesus* thus "articulates the strong sense of identification with Jesus that baptism generates."[19] Baptism therefore pronounces who we are and who we are called to be by articulating our affiliation with the Son.

This affiliation is unlike any other we have. To be baptized into Christ is to have our whole being and existence constituted in him and thus governed by him. Paul tells us that "all of us who have been

15 John C. Clark and Marcus Peter Johnson, *A Call to Christian Formation: How Theology Makes Sense of Our World* (Grand Rapids, MI: Baker Academic, 2021), 99.

16 Packer, *Concise Theology*, 224.

17 See Sinclair B. Ferguson, "Infant Baptism View," in Wright, *Baptism*, 92.

18 Scot McKnight, *It Takes a Church to Baptize: What the Bible Says about Infant Baptism* (Grand Rapids, MI: Brazos, 2018), 50; Macaskill, *Living in Union with Christ*, 60.

19 Macaskill, *Living in Union with Christ*, 60.

baptized into Christ Jesus were baptized into his death," so that "just as Christ was raised from the dead by the glory of the Father, we too might walk in newness of life" (Rom. 6:3–4). Baptism—both submersion in and emergence from water[20]—signifies not death and resurrection generically but death and resurrection *in Christ*. To be baptized into Christ, therefore, is to be identified with *his* death and *his* resurrection and to have his story of humiliation, suffering, death, and resurrection determine our personal narratives and identities.[21] Baptism teaches us that our lives now follow the pattern or trajectory of his. Immersion into Christ, therefore, changes the very structure, shape, meaning, and purpose of our lives.[22]

To have our lives follow the pattern of Christ's is to have our very selves reconfigured. This reconfiguring does not consist in reorientation on our part, some sort of self-initiated shift in perspective or self-determined alteration of lifestyle. It consists in death to self and the birth of a new self.

First, we learn from Paul that our "old self" has been crucified with Christ (Rom. 6:6). In the context of Romans 6, the old self is associated with "the body of sin." Elsewhere, Paul describes the old self by its "practices," which are "earthly"—that is, characteristic of the world and opposed to heavenly things, things characteristic of God's kingdom—and thus arouse God's anger (Col. 3:5–9; cf. Eph. 4:22). But the old self is more than simply sinful actions because Paul distinguishes between the old self and its practices

---

20 While *baptisma* means "immersion," immersion is not the only appropriate mode of baptism. Pouring and sprinkling, which have significant biblical and historical precedent, are also recognized by various Christian traditions as suitable modes, though undoubtedly immersion has certain symbolic advantages. For a helpful discussion, see Vos, *Reformed Dogmatics*, 965–70.

21 Macaskill, *Living in Union with Christ*, 65.

22 Cf. Michael J. Gorman, *Participating in Christ: Explorations in Paul's Theology and Spirituality* (Grand Rapids, MI: Baker Academic, 2019), 20.

("the old self *with its practices*," Col. 3:9).[23] While the two are necessarily connected, the former cannot be reduced to or defined solely by the latter. For Paul, something more powerful motivates and engenders our habits and actions. The old self is therefore the ethically degenerative part of who we are that is enslaved to sin, the "bundle of attitudes and emotions and practices" that we are apart from Christ,[24] which is what Paul is likely getting at in Ephesians 4:22 when he states that the "old self . . . is *corrupt through deceitful desires*." Part and parcel of this mass of attitudes and actions is self-reference, self-reliance, and self-preoccupation, a disposition that resists God and operates under the delusion that we are lords of our lives and thus ultimately responsible for charting our life courses and creating our own moralities. Regarding identity, it presupposes that we are individuals capable of determining our meaning, purpose, and significance in life and that the nature of our true selves is defined by our personal narratives and achievements or any other distinctive qualities we have. The old self assumes autonomy from God and others and is enslaved to sin and its practices, and it disorders the significance of our personal particularities. But this old self is buried in baptism, drowned in the watery tomb. We, who are sinful and have a distorted outlook on life—especially on our own selves and capabilities—have been put to death in baptism.

Second, having our lives, our very selves, reconfigured also involves resurrection. The baptismal font, therefore, is not just a *tomb* in which our old selves are buried and left to rot but also a *womb* from which our new selves emerge.[25] That last statement

---

23 John Piper, "Put on the New Person," Desiring God, September 21, 1986, https://www.desiringgod.org/.

24 Piper, "Put on the New Person."

25 See Jean Daniélou, *The Bible and the Liturgy* (Notre Dame, IN: University of Notre Dame Press, 1956), 47–49.

is undoubtedly provocative for many Christians today, but it is one affirmed early in the history of the church and connected to the idea of the church as mother. One of the most succinct and famous statements in this regard comes from Cyprian: "He can no longer have God for his Father, who has not the Church for his mother."[26] As I explained in the previous chapter, the Christian faith is inherited, and no one comes to faith in the crucified and risen Lord apart from others. The church, therefore, is the living organism that God uses to draw persons to himself—or, to use more personal imagery, she is the mother by which the children of God are born into new life. Speaking of the church, Calvin states,

> Let us learn even from the simple title "mother" how useful, indeed how necessary, it is that we should know her. For there is no other way to enter into life unless this mother conceive us in her womb, give us birth, nourish us at her breast, and lastly, unless she keep us under her care and guidance until, putting off mortal flesh, we become like the angels.[27]

And so baptism is the entry rite of mother church whereby repentant sinners are incorporated into Christ's body, ushered into God's family. Thus the quote often attributed to Didymus the Blind: "The baptismal pool is the workshop of the Trinity for the salvation of all faithful people. . . . She [the church] becomes the mother of all by the Holy Spirit while remaining a Virgin."[28] In no way does this trivialize or dismiss divine agency in conversion and

---

26 Cyprian, *On the Unity of the Church*, in *ANF* 5:423 (1.6).

27 Calvin, *Inst.*, 4.1.4.

28 Didymus the Blind, *De Trinitate*, ed. J.-P. Migne, PG 39 (Paris: Migne, 1858), 691, translated and quoted in Daniélou, *The Bible and the Liturgy*, 48; translation slightly altered. The treatise *De Trinitate* is often attributed to Didymus, yet scholars debate whether he is its author.

regeneration. God is ultimately the one who draws persons to himself and grants them new life by his Spirit, yet in his wisdom, he has seen fit to use the church as the organism by which he vivifies repentant sinners who were formerly dead in their trespasses.

Again, this new life we receive as baptized persons is not some generic revitalization. As Paul explains, because we have "died with Christ" (Rom. 6:8), we have also "been raised" with him (Col. 3:1)—this is baptismal imagery and language, mind you (cf. Col. 2:12; 3:1)—and we now share in *his* resurrection life. So significant is our participation in and accompaniment with Christ in his resurrection that our life is now "hidden" in him. Our whole being is enveloped into his, so much so that *he is our life* (Col. 3:1–4). And if he is our life, then we must affirm with Paul that "it is no longer *I* who live, but *Christ* who lives in me" (Gal. 2:20). This means we discern *our identity* aright only in relation to *his identity, our selves* in relation to *his self*.[29] Or as Julie Canlis explains, relaying Calvin's thought, "God and the self cannot be known in isolation, either through introspection or abstraction, but only as they are *in relation* to one another."[30] The self can be known only in God's presence, and specifically *in Christ*.[31] In fact, as those baptized into Christ, we cannot even separate our "identity from being 'in Christ.'"[32]

This does not mean that we as particular persons cease to exist the moment we come to faith in Christ and are baptized into him. Instead, it means that our own personal achievements, narratives,

29 This expression is informed by a personal conversation with John C. Clark.
30 Julie Canlis, "John Calvin: Knowing the Self in God's Presence," in *Sources of the Christian Self: A Cultural History of Christian Identity*, ed. James M. Houston and Jens Zimmermann (Grand Rapids, MI: Eerdmans, 2018), 407; emphasis original.
31 Canlis, "Knowing the Self," 408, 410.
32 Canlis, "Knowing the Self," 410.

relationships, possessions, and any other identity markers we might pinpoint as somehow determinative for who we are do not actually define the limits of our existence or constitute the structure of our true selves.[33] Put differently, the particular features of ourselves that distinguish us from others (see Gal. 3:28) are not obliterated but reordered and redefined the moment we are baptized into Christ.[34] Christ is our identity, our life, because we are in him and he is in us. He is both the *source* of our lives because he is the Creator and Sustainer of all things (Col. 1:16–17) and the *template* for our own personal lives because he is the "last Adam" (1 Cor. 15:45), the one who has inaugurated the new creation and is the archetype for new humanity. And as persons who belong to the new world order, we have a "new self" that is fashioned after the likeness of Christ (Col. 3:10). We have even "put on Christ" (Gal. 3:27), meaning that we have been donned with his very identity. Thus Calvin can state, in commenting on our baptism into Christ's death and resurrection, "We not only derive the strength and sap of the life which flows from Christ, but we also *pass from our own nature into his.*"[35]

Baptism—which, again, is something from God to us, not the inverse—reinforces the truth that our identity is not self-generated or determined ultimately by our own personal narratives and achievements or by our failures, mistakes, and unmet expectations. Nor is our identity reduced to the basic elements that distinguish us from others, as significant as those may be. Rather, our identity as persons in Christ, no less our very existence, is a gift from God, determined ultimately by Christ's life story and his accomplishments.

---

33 Macaskill, *Living in Union with Christ*, 53.

34 Macaskill, *Living in Union with Christ*, 56.

35 John Calvin, *The Epistles of Paul the Apostle to the Romans and to the Thessalonians*, ed. David W. Torrance and Thomas F. Torrance, trans. Ross Mackenzie, CNTC 8 (Grand Rapids, MI: Eerdmans, 1960), 124 (on Rom. 6:5); emphasis added.

And because baptism is never depicted in the New Testament as an optional rite left to the conscience of the individual, we who profess Christ must be identified with him in the fullest sense, meaning that all of who we are must be conformed to him and his life story.

A New Status

What, then, does this new God-given and Christ-determined identity entail? First, a change in status. As I stated above, we as baptized persons have entered an entirely new existence in the Son and have been granted his identity, though in a way that does not obliterate our individuality or make us ontologically homogeneous with him. In our union with Christ, the personal and Creator-creature distinctions are retained. We are personally distinct from Christ, God the Son, yet reconciled and united to him in a spiritually one-flesh manner[36]—like a man and woman become one flesh in marriage but remain personally distinct. We are creatures still, finite and capable of sin, yet our immersion into him means we no longer belong to the world and instead belong to the triune God and his family (see Gal. 4:1–7).

Union with Christ the Son therefore results in reunion with the Father. Again, to be baptized in the name of someone is to come into close relational existence with that person. We are baptized into Christ Jesus, which means we are baptized into the name of the triune God because it is through Christ, to whom we are united by the Spirit, that we have access to the Father. By virtue of our immersion into the Son, his Father is now our Father, and we have been granted his sonly identity—though he is the only "begotten"

36 As we pray in my own tradition just before receiving Communion, "Grant us, therefore, gracious Lord, so to eat the flesh of your dear Son Jesus Christ, and to drink his blood, *that our sinful bodies may be made clean by his body.*" BCP 119.

Son of the Father, meaning that we are adopted sons in him.[37] Thus Luther can say in one breath, "I am a son of God, I am baptized." To be baptized into Christ is to share in the sonship of Christ. Baptism, therefore, signifies and seals our adoption to be children of the Father (Gal. 3:26–27).[38] Whatever else we may say about immersion into Christ and having our existence and identity constituted in him, we must, without a hint of equivocation, say this: We are children of the Father because we have been granted the filial identity of the Son. To be in the Son is to be a son. And to be in the Son who is eternally begotten of the Father is to be a son now and forevermore and to be a coheir with him, our elder brother. What he has by rights as the Son of God by nature and as the result of his redemptive-historical work, we have by grace as sons of God by adoption. To those inextricably united to him, he has given that which is his, and he will not revoke it.

I acknowledge that some readers may be troubled by the application of masculine language to all believers, and this might seem problematic in a book on identity since such usage might seem to dishonor one's God-given gender or obliterate the personhood of females. It is vital, however, to understand that our identity as Christians is contingent on Christ's *sonly* relationship to the Father. While certain Scripture passages indeed refer to believers as "children" of God (e.g., John 1:12; Rom. 8:16–17; Phil. 2:14), here I emphasize the gendered term "son," which Paul uses in an inclusive rather than an exclusive manner and applies to all believers, regardless of their biological sex (see Rom. 8:14–15, 19, 23; Gal. 3:7, 26; 4:5–6; Eph. 1:5). As Macaskill explains, "It

---

37 On the significance of understanding our sonly identity as persons in Christ, see David B. Garner, *Sons in the Son: The Riches and Reach of Adoption in Christ* (Phillipsburg, NJ: P&R, 2016), 51–54; Macaskill, *Living in Union with Christ*, 98.

38 See Thirty-Nine Articles, art. 27 (*CCC* 126).

is important that we retain this gendered dimension . . . because it expresses our identity as God's adopted children specifically with reference to our participation in the Son. That is, the gendered particularity is a function of the personal particularity of the one *in whom* we are saved."[39] Moreover, when Paul applies the male term "sons" (Gk. *huioi*) to *all Christians*, he is saying that females and males share equally in Christ's sonship.[40] Their status before the Father is identical, though their particularities differ from each other.

It may be helpful to briefly note that while both males and females were adopted in Greco-Roman society, males were preferred adoptees since they could continue the family line and females could not.[41] Moreover, while women could technically be heirs in Roman law (even with their limited rights in comparison to men), it seems unlikely that adopted women in this context had access to the inheritance.[42] This means that Paul's thought countered cultural practices at the time. The scope of salvation applies to both males and females. Both are adopted by God and participate in Christ's sonship, and both are coheirs with him. Males and females have equal access to a shared inheritance in Christ. There is truly neither male nor female when it comes to being a child of God

39 Macaskill, *Living in Union with Christ*, 63n2; emphasis original.

40 As James Scott explains, "[Second] Corinthians 6:18, under the influence of Isaiah 43:6, explicitly broadens the concept of adoption to 'daughters.' Hence both males and females are included in Paul's concept of divine 'sonship.'" James M. Scott, "Adoption, Sonship," in *Dictionary of Paul and His Letters*, ed. Gerald F. Hawthorne, Ralph A. Martin, and Daniel G. Reid (Downers Grove, IL: InterVarsity Press, 1993), 18. Or as David Garner remarks, "The selection of 'son' (*huios*) or 'sons' (*huioi*) serves Paul's purpose to expose the inviolable, indissoluble filial solidarity of the redeemed with the Redeemer." Garner, *Sons in the Son*, 53.

41 Trevor J. Burke, *Adopted into God's Family: Exploring a Pauline Metaphor*, NSBT 22 (Downers Grove, IL: IVP Academic, 2006), 21n2.

42 See E. A. Castelli, "Romans," in *Searching the Scriptures*, vol. 2, *A Feminist Commentary*, ed. Elisabeth Schüssler Fiorenza (New York: Crossroad, 1994), 291, cited in Burke, *Adopted into God's Family*, 73n3.

and receiving an inheritance in Christ. Paul's concept of adoption therefore subverts cultural norms and shows just how radically countercultural the gospel is.

All Christians, regardless of their biological sex, are thus part of true Israel, God's "firstborn son" (Ex. 4:22), and are "sons of Abraham" (Gal. 3:7) by virtue of their immersion into Christ, the eternally and only begotten Son of the Father, who is himself true Israel and *the* promised seed of Abraham.[43] This application of specific gendered language, therefore, should not offend us but delight us. Nor should it trouble us given that the feminine term "bride" is also applied to collective believers, regardless of our biological sex as particular persons (Rev. 19:7; 21:2, 9; 22:17; cf. Eph. 5:22–23, where Paul refers to the church as Christ's bride, and 2 Cor. 11:2, where he describes the Corinthian Christians as a virgin betrothed to Christ).

While our adoption as sons in the Son is certainly a forensic or legal reality, it is not merely so, as Paul intimates in Galatians 4.[44] Our change in status to the Father is grounded in the Son's relation to him. Indeed, our adoption is a Trinitarian reality, the work of the Father, Son, and Spirit. The Father sends the Son to become one with us in our humanity and accomplish our salvation, and the Spirit applies the salvation accomplished by the Son to those who have faith in him, thus making us children of the Father who receive all the benefits secured by Christ, our elder brother and coheir (see Rom. 8:17). Moreover, it is the Spirit who causes us, those baptized into and donned with Christ, to cry out with the

---

43 While God the Son became man and thus a (male) sexed being in his humanity, God in his essence is not sexed and therefore is not male. God has, however, revealed himself as Father, Son, and Holy Spirit. The gendered terms therefore reveal something vital about the particularities of the persons of the Trinity, and we ought not discard them.

44 See Macaskill, *Living in Union with Christ*, 98–100.

Son to the Father with intimate and familial language (Rom. 8:17; Gal. 4:7). It is the Son's very cry that we utter: the Spirit *of the Son* is sent into our hearts, and he cries out through us, "Abba! Father!" (Gal. 4:6).[45] And the Father exuberantly welcomes such familial language because he hears us in his Son, the one in whom we live by faith. Therefore, any doubts we have about the Father and his tender love and compassion for us—perhaps influenced by tragic experiences with an earthly parent—can be eroded by the promises signified and sealed in baptism.[46] The Father who expressed his love for and delight in his only and eternally begotten Son at the Jordan has chosen to lavish on us that same paternal love and delight because we have been baptized into his Son and therefore adopted in him. As those who have been stripped of the old self and clothed with the new self that is fashioned after the Son, we are loved by the Father *even as he loves the Son* (John 17:23).

This reality has profound implications for the way we view ourselves and our personal relationships. We are social beings, and our identities are formed by our relationships with others. As David Jopling puts it, "Persons come to know themselves in being known by and responsive to persons other than themselves."[47] Or as Charles Taylor explains, "One is a self only among other selves. A self can

---

45 Macaskill, *Living in Union with Christ*, 98.

46 In no way am I suggesting that uncertainty over God's paternal love for us can be easily removed or that baptism immediately assuages doubts, anxiety, and fear. Many Christians struggle long and hard to understand and experience the Father's love for them because their relationship with their own father or mother is unstable or unloving. Therefore, discerning and diligent catechesis and counsel, guided by and fortified with prayer, are required to help such Christians understand and receive the gift of the Father's love for them. Nevertheless, when the promises signified and sealed in baptism are understood more deeply and embraced more firmly, we experience more joy and tranquility in knowing the Father's love for us. And laying hold of such promises is a continual exercise that is enabled by prayer, Scripture reading, fellowship, service, and, of course, participation in the sacraments.

47 David A. Jopling, *Self-Knowledge and the Self* (New York: Routledge, 2000), 166.

never be described without reference to those who surround it."[48] Personal identity is revealed and enacted in community. The adoption rite of baptism teaches us that we are loved and known by God the Father.[49] Even when we feel unseen or ignored by others, we can have confidence that we are seen by God and are known by him because we are in his Son. Even when others are callous toward us or withdrawn from us, for whatever reason, we can have confidence that the Father has drawn near to us and set his paternal affection on us in Christ. In fact, because we are in his Son, we exist where he is. The apostle John tells us that Jesus is at the Father's side—literally, in the bosom of the Father (John 1:18). Because of our immersion into the Son, we too are at the Father's side. As Michael Reeves so wonderfully states, "When the Son takes his beloved one into his bosom (13:23), he brings [believers] with him where he is (17:24): in the bosom of the Father."[50] We are like an infant who is held secure, lovingly and tenderly, at the breast of his mother and nourished to experience life and joy by her affection and care. Our proximity to the Father, by virtue of our inextricable union with the Son by the Spirit, produces unrivaled and unending bliss because we participate in the eternal delight that the three persons of the Trinity share for one another as the God of love.

Christians therefore do not need to look far—and especially do not need to turn to the world and those of it—for acceptance. One feeling that the promises signified and sealed in baptism mitigate is anxiety over how others view us and whether they will accept us.

---

48 Charles Taylor, *Sources of the Self: The Making of the Modern Identity* (Cambridge, MA: Harvard University Press, 1989), 35.

49 For a wonderful discussion of identity and being known by God, see Brian Rosner, *How to Find Yourself: Why Looking Inward Is Not the Answer* (Wheaton, IL: Crossway, 2022), chap. 7.

50 Michael Reeves, *Gospel People: A Call for Evangelical Integrity* (Wheaton, IL: Crossway, 2022), 48. Cf. Isa. 40:11.

Many of us have felt the weight of worrying what others think of us, to the point that we constantly attempt to keep up appearances and meet the standards of others and ourselves—which are often unrealistic, twisted, or arbitrary—to be esteemed and approved. Yet when we lay hold of the promises extended to us in baptism, we are assured that by virtue of our immersion into Christ, we are acceptable in the eyes of the Father as his children, even when we do not feel we are so. How can this be? Because Christ "was delivered up for our trespasses and raised for our justification" (Rom. 4:25).

Throughout history, and no less today, many people believe—either in theory or in practice—that their salvation is produced by their own good works. To be accepted by God, one must perform certain deeds and abstain from others. The gospel confronts this notion by exposing our inability to make ourselves righteous and acceptable before God and by shifting our focus from ourselves to another who is wholly righteous and acceptable to God—his Son, Jesus Christ. As Calvin explains, justification—one of the benefits given to us in union with Christ—is "the acceptance with which God receives us into his favor as righteous," and it consists in the forgiveness of sins and imputation of Christ's righteousness.[51] Because we are united to Christ by Spirit-created faith, the Father does not see our sins or shortcomings and instead sees only the goodness and purity of his Son. Baptism assures us of this reality because it signifies and seals our justification in Christ alone by faith alone—that God, based on Christ's work and not ours, has removed our sins from us (Acts 2:38; 22:16) and imputed Christ's righteousness to us. Even when our past sins and mistakes seem to be always before us, we may be assured that in the divine reality all

51 Calvin, *Inst.*, 3.11.2.

our faults have been washed away from God's sight and we have been clothed with Christ, the righteous one (Gal. 3:27).

This cleansing is what Peter has in mind when he declares, "Baptism, which corresponds to [the flood], now saves you, not as a removal of dirt from the body but as an appeal to God for a good conscience, through the resurrection of Jesus Christ" (1 Pet. 3:21). Baptism itself does not save us *ex opere operato* (from the work performed), but God uses the sacrament of water to save us by purging the conscience of dead works, just as he used the flood to rid the earth of evil.[52] To God, our sins are truly out of sight, out of mind. To those of us who belong to the new covenant, of which baptism is the initiatory rite, God declares, "I will forgive their iniquity, and I will remember their sin no more" (Jer. 31:34; cf. Heb. 8:12; 10:17). He has "tread our iniquities underfoot" and "cast all our sins / into the depths of the sea" (Mic. 7:19). He not only destroys our faults and transgressions but hurls them into a watery grave from which they can never emerge. And when we rise from our tomb, the baptismal font, the Father declares that we are as clean as his Son, and the promises that he speaks over us are intended to purify our consciences of the sins that haunt us. As baptized persons, we are defined not by our sins or mistakes or failures, whether past or present, but by our existence in the Son, the righteous one in whom there is no fault.

This assurance relieves us of the fear of judgment and condemnation as well as the feeling that we need to justify ourselves before others. Because we are in Christ, God is to us a loving Father instead of a strict Judge, as Calvin puts it.[53] People may, and frequently

---

52 Peter J. Leithart, *Baptism: A Guide to Life from Death* (Bellingham, WA: Lexham, 2021), 35.
53 Calvin, *Inst.*, 3.11.1.

do, relate to us as rigorous judges, unfairly and often duplicitously demanding that we meet unrealistic or inappropriate standards or even that we signal some sort of supposed virtue to earn or keep their approval and acceptance. And if we do not meet their expectations, they may capriciously scrutinize, villainize, and ostracize us. But because Christ immersed himself into and endured human judgment and condemnation throughout his earthly life as well as divine judgment and condemnation at Golgotha, we will never suffer ultimate judgment and condemnation. God has canceled the record of debt against us (Col. 2:14), and therefore he will never cancel us. Any disapproval that others cast on us has no bearing on our status before the Father, and this truth produces such tranquility and joy that we can walk without fearing what others think of us and instead live others-centered lives, serving them and loving them as the Father has loved us in Christ.

Some voices, however, whether from within ourselves or from those around us, contradict this reality and even slander us, telling us that we are not forgiven or clean, that we are not approved, that we are worthless and unloved. It is for precisely such reasons that the Christian life is, to borrow Luther's concept, a perpetual baptism.[54] The promises that the Father speaks through the sacrament of water to us, his children, not only are applicable when we first turn to his Son in faith but cover our whole lives and therefore must be embraced continuously day after day. And as we, by the power of his Spirit, lay hold of these promises that we are adopted by the Father and accepted by him because we have been declared righteous on the basis of his Son's work alone, we come to realize

---

54 Martin Luther, "The Large Catechism," in *The Book of Concord: The Confessions of the Evangelical Lutheran Church*, ed. Robert Kolb and Timothy J. Wengert, trans. Charles Arand et al. (Minneapolis: Fortress, 2000), 445.

more who we are as in-Christ persons. We are persons of the water and the blood, cleansed and atoned for.

It is vital to understand, however, that our acceptance by the Father on the basis of Christ's atoning work is *not a validation of who we are*. God does not look at us and say we are fine as we are. Rather, he looks on us *as though we were his Son*—perfect, holy, righteous. And at the same time that he justifies us, he also sanctifies us. He therefore does not validate *us*. He does not care to confirm our feelings, which may or may not accord with reality and his truth, and he certainly does not affirm our sins. No, he makes a declaration in accord with his good and glorious will, and he calls us to new life in his Son that is marked by holiness. God does not act as our world does. He does not tolerate or even celebrate who *we* think we are or think we can be. Those whom he justifies he sanctifies, and he conforms us to the image *of his Son*. He gives us a new status and leads us to live in accord with that status.

A New People

Part of the new status we have been granted as persons immersed into Christ is our incorporation into a new people. We are adopted sons and daughters who belong to the family of God, and the adoption rite of baptism creates among us "a relation of *brotherly and sisterly union*, itself founded on a relation of *filiation* in him, the Son, through the Spirit."[55] Notice the plural in Paul's letter to the Galatians: "In Christ Jesus *you are all sons* of God" because "as many of you as were baptized into Christ have put on Christ" (Gal.

---

55 Louis-Marie Chauvet, *Symbol and Sacrament: A Sacramental Reinterpretation of Christian Existence*, trans. Patrick Madigan and Madeleine Beaumont (Collegeville, MN: Liturgical Press, 1995), 439–40.

3:26–27). Baptism, and the reality that it signifies and seals, is not a private or individual affair and does not lead us into a solitary existence. As Louis-Marie Chauvet explains,

> In putting on the same Christ in baptism, Christians become in effect members of this "one new humanity" and this "one body" Christ has formed in giving his life so that "the dividing wall" which separates humanity (for Paul, Jew and Gentile) might be destroyed (Eph. 2:14–16). Now, through baptism, it is this "new humanity" that comes forth according to the same Paul. We die there to the "old humanity" (the old collective "Adam," the one subject to the reign of sin) in order to put on the "new humanity" (the new collective "Adam" whose "corporate personality" Christ represents).[56]

While we as baptized persons are granted a new identity in Christ, that identity we receive is a collective one—this is why I have been continually saying "our identity" rather than "our identities" in Christ. We all have put on the same Christ, and by being united to the same Christ, we all are united to each other by the same Spirit.

It is for this reason that one cannot baptize oneself and that baptism is always performed in the company of believers gathered for worship of the triune God. Baptism is a corporate activity by which the recipient is ushered into the people of God, and all who are baptized into Christ are "baptized into one body" (1 Cor. 12:13), Christ's body. This apostolic truth is affirmed by the universal church and reflected in nearly every

---

56 Chauvet, *Symbol and Sacrament*, 440.

historical Protestant confession: baptism is the rite by which recipients "are grafted into the Church," as the Thirty-Nine Articles confesses.[57] Or to use Paul's formula in his letter to the Ephesians, "There is one body and one Spirit—just as you were called to the one hope that belongs to your call—one Lord, one faith, one baptism, one God and Father of all, who is over all and through all and in all" (Eph. 4:4–6). All who are in Christ possess the same faith (cf. 2 Pet. 1:1), and it is by faith that we are immersed into Christ and his body by the one Spirit and thus have God as our Father.

By nature, therefore, baptism *cannot be a solitary reality or event* because Christ, the one into whom we are immersed, is eternally, inextricably, and perichoretically[58] joined to the Father and Spirit and is by virtue of his incarnation and work of redemption joined inseparably as head to his body, the church, by the power and agency of the Spirit. Self-baptism is therefore a theological and ecclesial sham and perpetuates ungodly notions rampant in our culture, which place the self and its activity at the center of attention. The Trinitarian and ecclesial reality of baptism subverts perverted concepts of the self by reinforcing that we are not solitary, independent, and self-referential beings who generate our own personal identities, significance, and even morals in isolation from others. Signifying our entry into the church, the sacrament of water forces us to acknowledge that we are not mere individuals

57 Thirty-Nine Articles, art. 27 (*CCC* 126); see also, e.g., WCF 28.1 (*CCC* 228); Belgic Confession, art. 34 (*CCC* 105).

58 *Perichoresis* is a term used to describe the interpenetration and mutual indwelling—and thus the perfect and eternal unity, inseparability, and relationality—of the three persons of the Trinity. For a helpful discussion of perichoresis, see D. Glenn Butner Jr., *Trinitarian Dogmatics: Exploring the Grammar of the Christian Doctrine of God* (Grand Rapids, MI: Baker Academic, 2022), 133–52.

or isolated beings. Baptism in the name of the triune God forms not only new persons but also a new people.[59]

This means that the primary people group with whom we are to identify is the church, regardless of the other identity markers we and other members of Christ's body might have. To be human is to be *homo sociologicus*, a social person. As I have already iterated variously, we all are formed by our social roles and locations within communities. This means that, in the words of Michael Horton, "the 'self'—understood as an autonomous individual—does not exist, but is already bound up with tradition, history, and community."[60] Indeed, the autonomous self is a *false self*.[61] Many moderns presume that we as individuals are able to determine our existence without external constraints, but the truth is that we all are shaped profoundly by the groups with which we identify and to which we belong. Baptism does not deny this reality but immerses us into a new and altogether different society, the church, where what ultimately counts is not our particularities such as Jew or Greek, slave or free, male or female—to mention those most significant in Paul's day (Gal. 3:28). In baptism, the particularities of who we are, specifically the social positions and connections we have and so often cling to for personal meaning and significance, are completely relativized—and some, if ungodly and antagonistic toward our new identity in Christ, are mortified. As Peter Leithart states,

In baptism, fleshly identities—national, ethnic, familial, educational, economic—are submerged. All the baptized wear the

59 See Peter J. Leithart, *The Priesthood of the Plebs: A Theology of Baptism* (Eugene, OR: Wipf & Stock, 2003), chap. 5.
60 Michael Horton, *The Christian Faith: A Systematic Theology for Pilgrims on the Way* (Grand Rapids, MI: Zondervan, 2011), 87.
61 This pithy statement is informed by personal conversation with John C. Clark.

family name of "Father, Son, and Spirit," relativizing all other names—"American," "Smith," "Yale law grad." This is how baptism into . . . Christ makes us new creatures: it gives us a new identity and a new name, not of the flesh but of the Spirit.[62]

Because we now belong to a new people, a new humanity in which there are no dividing walls, "the identity of individuals is no longer exhausted by the social roles they happen to occupy." Put differently, "conventional social roles . . . become secondary in relation to" the "primary role shared equally by all" in Christ.[63] The identity markers of this world that are so precious in our sight are given new meaning—indeed, less significance—in baptism. When Paul tells the Galatians that there is neither Jew nor Greek, slave nor free, male nor female, he is not trivializing or dismissing the empirically obvious reality that their (and our) personal particularities, positions within larger society, and divinely granted genders still exist. His point is that while these remain, they are subordinated to our new, common identity as baptized persons who have been donned with Christ. And since all who have faith in Christ have been united to him, we all share a common identity and bond that make the church the group we are to primarily associate with. Those to whom we are united, as one body, by virtue of our immersion into the Son, are more our people than those who share our nationality, ethnicity, skin color, cultural context, educational background, economic status, political preferences, hobbies, and so on.

Granted, we as Christians naturally form special and intimate bonds with other Christians who have particularities similar to

---

62 Leithart, *Baptism*, 46.

63 Larry Siedentop, *Inventing the Individual: The Origins of Western Liberalism* (Cambridge, MA: Belknap Press of Harvard University Press, 2014), 62.

ours, and there is nothing wrong with this per se, so long as we do not elevate these particularities above our common identity as in-Christ persons or denigrate others in Christ who are different from us, depreciating our spiritual bond with them. As Brian Rosner states, "Baptism speaks of our shared memory and defining destiny that form our identity in Christ. We die with Christ to self-interest and self-assertion and we rise to new life now and most fully in the future."[64] This is true for us as particular persons and us as an entire people. In baptism, we are liberated from our own personal and group interests so that we may love and serve the entire body of which we are members. And again, it is this people group—the historic and universal church—that should shape and influence us most in comparison to other groups. And if any group's priorities do not align with those of Christ's body, then we need to rethink carefully our association with that group.[65]

More positively, as baptized persons, we have confidence that we belong: we belong to God the Father as his sons and daughters and to one another as brothers and sisters. This world is a lonely place for many, and people today are experiencing increasing levels of loneliness owing to, as one example, excessive use of technology, especially social media—which is ironic, because such means promise greater connectedness with others but ultimately fail to deliver what is best for us. Many of us are insecure in our relationships and are anxious about intimacy, and so we turn to technology for security and meaningful relationships.[66] What we get in return are

---

64 Rosner, *How to Find Yourself*, 195.

65 Numerous biblical proverbs speak to the importance, indeed necessity, of choosing wise counsel and godly relations if we are to persevere to everlasting life: e.g., Prov. 12:26; 13:20; 22:24–25; cf. Ps. 1:1; 1 Cor. 15:33.

66 Sherry Turkle, *Alone Together: Why We Expect More from Technology and Less from Each Other* (New York: Basic Books, 2017), xii.

counterfeit goods and experiences that lead us away from activities that are most satisfying relationally. Not to mention that technology often distracts us from those who are in our physical presence. This is not to say that technology is altogether evil, but we must recognize that the devices and media we so often turn to for reassurance and contentment—often unknowingly—cannot provide that for which we ultimately yearn. Another reason so many of us feel isolated and alone is that we are preoccupied with ourselves, attempting to discover ourselves and seek our own interests, which naturally takes our focus off others.[67]

No doubt, many other factors contribute to the high levels of isolation and loneliness in our age, and no matter what the source or cause of these ailments is for Christians, the water of baptism is an effective antidote. Baptism reorients our gaze, teaching us to look to the triune God for acceptance and belonging. When we look to the baptismal font, we are reminded that the triune God has freely accepted us and engrafted us into the church, the people group with whom we share a common bond, identity, and story in Christ. The baptized person is never an isolated person but rather one who is forever united to Christ and his body. We are *a people* of the water and the blood. We *as the church* are the bride taken from his side.

A New Creation

To be baptized into Christ is also to be made a new creation. This I have already touched on briefly when discussing the new self we become as a result of our immersion into and union with Christ. We are not just given a new status by being adopted as children

---

67 See Trevin Wax, "The Faithful Church in an Age of Expressive Individualism," *Kingdom People* (blog), The Gospel Coalition, October 22, 2018, https://www.thegospelcoalition .org/.

of the Father but are also made by the Spirit of the Son into new creatures who begin to act as those who belong to the divine family.[68] This is what numerous Protestant confessions get at when they speak of baptism as a sign and seal of regeneration or new birth.[69] To be baptized into Christ is to be baptized with the Holy Spirit, the Lord and giver of life, the "Sanctifier of the faithful."[70]

It should be clear by now, yet there is no risk in iterating more overtly: any benefit of salvation that we receive is by virtue of our union with Christ, who possesses in his very person and by way of his redemptive-historical activity that which he bestows on us. This means that we are baptized or endowed with the Holy Spirit because Christ was first baptized or endowed with the Spirit, which occurred at the Jordan in Jesus's inauguration into the messianic office. It is not as if Christ and the Spirit had no relationship prior to the Jordan but that in Jesus's baptism by John a "heightened stage of Spirit endowment" and a "new and deepened dimension in the relationship between Jesus and the Spirit" began for the sake of Christ's public ministry.[71] In several ways, Jesus's baptism in the Jordan is archetypal for our baptism as in-Christ persons. Just as Jesus was declared to be the Son of God and was approved by the Father, so are we declared to be sons, by adoption, and thus approved by him. But that is not all. As Richard Gaffin states, "What occurred at the Jordan has an integral bearing on the coming of

68 On the necessary conjunction of justification and sanctification under the rubric of adoption, see J. Todd Billings, *Union with Christ: Reframing Theology and Ministry for the Church* (Grand Rapids, MI: Baker Academic, 2011), 27–31.

69 See Thirty-Nine Articles, art. 27 (*CCC* 126); WCF 28.1 (*CCC* 228); Belgic Confession, art. 34 (*CCC* 106).

70 *BCP* 91, 649.

71 Richard B. Gaffin Jr., *In the Fullness of Time: An Introduction to the Biblical Theology of Acts and Paul* (Wheaton, IL: Crossway, 2022), 115. Cf. Ferguson, *Baptism in the Early Church*, 117.

the Spirit on the church at Pentecost, the church's baptism with the Holy Spirit."[72] As is recorded in John's Gospel, "He on whom you see the Spirit descend and remain, this is he who baptizes with the Holy Spirit" (John 1:33). And Gaffin further explains, "The heightening of this relationship reaches its consummate realization in the bond between Christ as resurrected and the Spirit."[73] The incarnate, crucified, resurrected, and ascended Messiah is so deeply and intimately joined to the Spirit that he became the last Adam and therefore the one who gives eschatological life (1 Cor. 15:45), which is signified and sealed in baptism.[74] What this means is that "Jesus is the Spirit-baptized and so, consequently, the Spirit-baptizing Christ."[75] To be baptized *into Christ* is to be baptized *with his Spirit*. Christ gives to his people that which is his by virtue of his messianic and redemptive work: life in the Spirit.

Those who have been baptized into and clothed with Christ are indwelt by the Holy Spirit—who is the Spirit of the Son, the Spirit of the resurrected Messiah, and therefore the giver of new life, Christ's life (Gal. 3:27–4:7).[76] The Spirit, who raised Jesus from the dead, grants those he inhabits the new life that is secured by Christ in his death and resurrection (Rom. 8:9–11). Again, this is not some generic new life but an entirely new existence that is constituted in and conformed to that of the crucified and risen Messiah. The new self is a self indwelt and animated by the Holy Spirit yet existing in union with the Son. This new self is therefore a new

---

72 Gaffin, *Fullness of Time*, 114. Ferguson states, "The declaration of Jesus' Sonship and the coming of the Holy Spirit on him at this time provide a parallel to the promises attached in a lesser sense to Christian baptism." Ferguson, *Baptism in the Early Church*, 100.

73 Gaffin, *Fullness of Time*, 115.

74 For helpful discussion of 1 Cor. 15:45, see Gaffin, *Fullness of Time*, chap. 12.

75 Gaffin, *Fullness of Time*, 114.

76 See Gorman, *Participating in Christ*, 106.

creation because it is now inhabited by the Spirit and conformed to the crucified and risen Lord, who by his redemptive-historical work has inaugurated a new world order.

We could explore much more about what the indwelling Spirit accomplishes, and later chapters address this topic. For now, it is sufficient to state that the Spirit who inhabits us, who regenerates us by granting us the life and filial identity of the crucified and risen Son, transfers us into wholly new existential territory. To be baptized into the Son, clothed with him, and filled with his Spirit means that we no longer belong to the world or the god of this world, Satan (John 12:31; 2 Cor. 4:4; 1 John 5:19). The vivifying and sanctifying Spirit with whom we are baptized in Christ rips us from the world and its "elementary principles" (Gal. 4:3). As Michael Gorman puts it, "Life in the Spirit of the crucified Messiah will therefore reflect the counterintuitive and countercultural ways of God" revealed in Christ.[77]

Baptism into Christ, the Spirit-baptizing Messiah, also brings about sanctified self-understanding, which certainly subverts worldly forms of self-understanding. The descent of the Spirit on Jesus and the Father's declaration over him at the Jordan was, as Everett Ferguson states, "no doubt significant for Jesus, for his self-consciousness and for the inauguration of his public life."[78] The event reassured Jesus not only of his mission but also of his sonship—though it would be godless conjecture to state that he was unaware of his sonly identity or mission prior to this event. This event parallels our own baptism into Christ. Baptism signifies and seals our adoption as sons and reception of the Holy Spirit. And a primary task of the indwelling Spirit is to bear "witness with our

---

77 Gorman, *Participating in Christ*, 113–14.
78 Ferguson, *Baptism in the Early Church*, 103.

spirit that we are children of God" (Rom. 8:16). The Spirit with whom we are baptized therefore strengthens our self-consciousness as children of the Father. Many people today are confused regarding who they are because they are not in Christ and therefore are not children of God. As those baptized into Christ, however, we never need to doubt who we truly are because the same Spirit who descended on Jesus when the Father declared his paternal love for him resides in our hearts and assures us that we are beloved children of the Father. And such certain self-awareness shapes our behavior.

Baptism into Christ liberates us to be and act like children of the Father and not slaves of the world and its god. Again, when we pass through the waters of baptism by faith, we are initiated into God's family. We are no longer estranged orphans but are adopted sons of the Father. And as those who are baptized into Christ and with the Spirit, we are enabled by the Spirit to act like the Son, who is now our life. This is the indicative of baptism: we have entered the new world order in Christ. And here is the imperative of baptism: we are to act as those who belong to the new world order in Christ. Paul exhorts, "Walk by the Spirit" (Gal. 5:16). And if we "live by the Spirit," we should "keep in step with the Spirit" (Gal. 5:25), meaning that we should manifest the fruit of the Spirit as those who belong to Christ (Gal. 5:22–24). To be baptized into Christ, clothed with him, and indwelt by his Spirit therefore leads us to renounce "the works of the flesh" (Gal. 5:19) and live according to the "law of Christ" (Gal. 6:2)—that is, our life pattern is and should be conformed to the life pattern of Christ.[79] This undoubtedly entails renouncing practices such as those listed in Galatians 5:19–21; Ephesians 4:19; and Colossians 3:8–9, but it includes far

79 See Gorman, *Participating in Christ*, 107.

more. Again, Paul distinguishes between the old self and its practices. Therefore, we are to renounce not just sinful practices that reflect the elementary principles of the world but also the world itself and its diabolical ruler. And this is possible because our old self has been crucified in Christ, drowned in the watery tomb of baptism, and we have been given a new self in resurrection with Christ. As Alexander Schmemann states, baptism renounces "an entire 'worldview' made up of pride and self-affirmation which has truly taken human life from God and made it into darkness, death and hell" and "is a profession of a personal attachment to Christ" and therefore "an enrollment in the ranks of those who serve Christ, of an oath similar to the one taken by soldiers."[80]

As those baptized into Christ and with his Spirit, we therefore inhabit and enact an existence entirely different from those belonging to the world. As Mark Sayers astutely observes, "individual freedom, happiness, self-definition, and self-expression" are of maximal significance in our world today. Anyone or anything that would restrict these must be rejected outrightly, "for the primary social ethic is tolerance of everyone's self-defined quest for individual freedom and self-expression. Any deviation from this ethic of tolerance is dangerous and must not be tolerated."[81] Baptism, however, represents an alternate and more satisfying reality—indeed, reality itself. The font teaches us that we are not inherently free and that

---

80 Alexander Schmemann, *Of Water and the Spirit: A Liturgical Study of Baptism* (Crestwood, NY: St. Vladimir's Seminary Press, 1974), 30, 31.

81 Mark Sayers, *Disappearing Church: From Cultural Relevance to Gospel Resilience* (Chicago: Moody Publishers, 2016), 17. Since Sayers published his work, the culture today has shifted to demanding more ardently not just toleration but affirmation and celebration of everyone's self-defined quest for individual freedom and self-expression. On this development, see Carl R. Trueman, *Strange New World: How Thinkers and Activists Redefined Identity and Sparked the Sexual Revolution* (Wheaton, IL: Crossway, 2022), esp. 87–88, 156–57.

individual freedom is not something to which we should aspire. Apart from Christ, who is the only truly free human, we are in bondage to sin and death. We need the power of Christ by his Spirit to liberate us from the tyranny of sin and Satan. And if the "self" is in such a wretched state apart from Christ, why would we want self-definition and self-expression? Who wants to be defined by bondage and death? Rather, baptism declares to us that the highest good in life is to be defined by Christ—the one in whom we are adopted, justified, sanctified—and to express him.

An Eschatological Self

This new self that is defined by and expresses Christ, however, is a progressive self, a self in process—it is moving toward its final goal and not yet what it ought to be.[82] As a rite exhibiting our union with Christ, baptism also signifies "resurrection unto everlasting life,"[83] an event for which we long with hope, gratitude, and joyful expectation—as well as with godly sorrow over present conditions (see Rom. 7–8). The new self that we have received and indeed become through baptism into Christ is not yet what it should or will be because our union with Christ, while real and secure now, is incomplete—in the sense that we have not yet been made fully like him. Or as Macaskill puts it, "Our baptism is linked to this putting off and putting on the old and new identities, but the identities themselves exist between the already and the not yet."[84] While our old self was crucified with Christ in baptism and we are no longer enslaved to sin and death (Rom. 6:6), we still wrestle with their residual effects (Rom. 7:14–25) because we have not

82 See Billings, *Union with Christ*, 31–34.
83 Westminster Larger Catechism q. 165 (hereafter cited as WLC) (*CCC* 395).
84 Macaskill, *Living in Union with Christ*, 107.

yet experienced "the redemption of our bodies" (Rom. 8:23). Paul connects our bodily redemption with our "adoption as sons" (Rom. 8:23), meaning that our adoption into God's family is in some sense an eschatological or a future reality. Yet in the same passage he declares that we are already children of God because the Spirit of the Son lives in us and has made us heirs with Christ (Rom. 8:16–17). Our very identity as children of the Father is a now-and-not-yet reality, a future reality that we experience and live out in part in the present.[85]

The new self, therefore, is not fully formed because it is not yet fully conformed to the Son in his bodily resurrection. We will be complete when he appears to us in the flesh, for on that day we will be like him because we will see him for who he is (1 John 3:2).[86] Baptism therefore signifies not just spiritual resurrection with Christ, in which we are liberated from the tyranny of sin and Satan and made coheirs with Christ as adopted children of the Father, but also physical resurrection, in which we will receive a body like that of our crucified, resurrected, and ascended Lord and possess the full inheritance of those who have received the sonly identity of the one who is eternally beloved of the Father.

It is vital to understand, therefore, that our new self is united not just to the historical Christ but also to the eschatological Christ, the Christ who sits in glory at the right hand of the Father (Col. 3:1). And because we are united to the ascended Christ, we too are raised up—again, this is resurrection and therefore baptismal language—and sit in the heavenly places with him (Eph. 2:6),

---

85 See Billings, *Union with Christ*, 31.

86 We are reminded of the power of sight. When we behold that which is ungodly, we are deformed by and into what we see. But when we behold that which is good and glorious, we are transformed by and into what we see. In the case of 1 John 3, when we look physically on the resurrected Christ, our bodies will be transformed into bodies like his.

spiritually though not yet physically. So as persons baptized into the crucified and risen Lord, we live eschatologically—that is, with the future being a reality in part for us in the present—because we are united to the historical and eschatological Christ, who is one and the same.

In the time between these two resurrections, the spiritual and the physical, we continue to experience the lingering effects of the fall. Our own failures and present circumstances in this broken world prevent us from fully understanding and enacting who we have become and will be in Christ. Many of us struggle to understand who we are because we live in such a sin-ridden world and because our failures blind us from the reality that, by virtue of our immersion into Christ, we have been made children of the Father and are accepted and loved freely by him. One strength of baptism as a sign and seal of the gospel is that it forces us to look not at ourselves and our failures but to Christ and his majestic work and to acknowledge with faith that "it is no longer I who live, but Christ who lives in me" (Gal. 2:20). As baptized persons who have been buried with Christ and raised with him to new life, and as persons who await the redemption of our bodies, we can have confidence that no matter how much we may fail morally, how much confusion we may experience over who we are, we are inextricably united to the Son and have received his glorious identity. And by the power of the Spirit, we can live according to who God has declared us to be rather than according to our vacillating feelings.

Baptism therefore reveals who we are and will be in Christ. It perpetually reminds us that we belong to the triune God and his family, have been refashioned after the image of Christ the Son, and have been given all the benefits he has secured for us in his redemptive-historical work. If we want to know more securely who we are, we would be wise to look to the baptismal font, which pronounces to us who Christ is and who we are in him. But we must be connected to the church to truly understand and be transformed by these truths. The sacrament of baptism is not solitary but connected to Communion, meaning not only that we cannot receive baptism apart from the communion of saints, the church, but also that we cannot enact our identity as baptized persons apart from that saintly communion. As John Zizioulas explains, "It is not an accident that our Lord uses the term 'Baptism' in connection with his death (Mt. 20:22; cf. Luke 12:50). The 'cup' of his death and the 'Baptism' of his death to which he refers there, can hardly be understood apart from the cup of the New Covenant of the Last Supper."[87] If we wish to understand and live out more fully who we are—to live out the reality of our baptism—we must understand and embrace that we as baptized persons are necessarily and unequivocally communing persons. We are immersed into Christ, and by virtue of our union with him, we commune with the triune God and his people. We are persons of the water *and the blood*. For that reason, our discussion of who we are in Christ is incomplete until we consider what Communion signifies and seals.

---

87 John D. Zizioulas, "Some Reflections on Baptism, Confirmation and Eucharist," *Sobornost* 5, no. 9 (1969): 646.

4

Communing Persons

IT IS NOT UNCOMMON for many of us today to feel, at some point in our lives, that we have lost our sense of self. Difficult or changing life circumstances, a transition from one life phase to another, shattered dreams, unmet expectations, new responsibilities, broken or lost relationships, trauma—all these and more can cause us to forget who we are or thought we were. As a result, we question our identity, what our purpose is, and whether our life is meaningful—or at least as meaningful as it could be. Our sense of satisfaction wanes, and sometimes we develop unhealthy habits to cope with our disappointments and frustrations. Even our relationships suffer. We seek approval from others in a detrimental manner, thus burdening those we look to for reassurance. And so we struggle to develop and maintain solid bonds with others when our own sense of self has deteriorated, for we cannot be who we are meant to be in relation to others when we are not personally thriving and when we are self-focused and bound by despair.

As Christians, it is easy to forget who we are in Christ. We are finite creatures who still wrestle with the presence of sin in our lives, and the cumulative effect of our creatureliness and sinfulness is that we often lose sight, even if momentarily, of who we are as persons baptized into Christ. Modern psychology often prescribes various methods of self-care or self-help to remedy a lost sense of self, but Christian identity cannot be maintained and developed through self-referential means. Our identity as Christians is generated by an extrinsic reality and so must be ratified by the same. To remember who we are as in-Christ persons, we need external reminders of what it means to be persons immersed into him and his body, the church. Self-help and self-care cannot bolster the Christian self. Therefore, to hold fast to who we are in Christ, who we were made and called to be in baptism, we must hold fast to Christ himself. We must look on *him*, take *him*, receive *him*. And this we do when we participate in the sacrament of his body and blood.

Baptism is the onetime sacrament of our immersion into Christ—literally the incorporation of our bodies into his body, of our selves into his very self—and therefore the sacrament of new identity in him. Communion, moreover, is the sacrament of our on-going participation in Christ, whereby we remember and commune with him and in doing so continually enact the identity we have received in him. To be clear, the sacrament of bread and wine is not primarily about us but about our gracious Lord, who gave himself for us and continuously gives himself to us. But as we receive his body and blood, not only is our faith in him strengthened, but so is our understanding of what it means to live in union and communion with him. As a result, we ourselves are nurtured—indeed, we grow into greater maturity in him—and therefore come to realize increasingly who we are as persons existing in him. Communion is therefore a meal whereby we remember who Christ is and what he has done for us, as well as who we are in him. Thus, it is a ritual whereby we identify with and participate in a reality far greater than ourselves, and as we do so, we are increasingly transformed into the likeness of our crucified and risen Lord. Put differently, in Communion, the identity that we have received in baptism is maintained and developed.

Commemorating Beings

In discovering how Communion leads us to remember who we are as baptized persons and how it helps us embody the identity we have received in Christ, it is fitting to begin our discussion of the meal by focusing on its commemorative nature. Any Christian celebrating Communion knows it is an act whereby we remember our crucified and risen Lord. When instituting the meal, Jesus himself commanded us to eat and drink in remembrance of him (Luke 22:19), and nearly every Protestant confession states that we commemorate Christ's sacrificial death in this meal. But this meal cannot be reduced to mere recollection of events. So in thinking about this meal, especially how it shapes our self-consciousness as in-Christ persons, the question is not whether our eating and drinking is commemorative but what the nature of our commemoration is. Are we simply pondering past events, or are we doing something greater? In chapter 2, we discovered that the sacraments are not just commemorative acts and that even as commemorative acts, they are more than intellectual exercises; they are identity-forming rituals because memory and identity are inextricably linked. When we are baptized into Christ by faith, we receive a new identity, his sonly identity, and so become an entirely new creature. In Communion, that identity is enacted, fortified, and even advanced.

From a redemptive-historical standpoint, the sacrament of bread and wine forms identity because it is analogous to the Passover, a ritual feast whereby the Israelites not only meditated on God's saving activity but also ratified their identity, both collectively and personally, as God's people.[1] Even though families after the exodus generation did not live under the tyranny of Pharaoh and experience firsthand liberation from his cruelty, the exodus story is all Israel's story by virtue of the people's identification with the exodus generation. Commenting on the institution of the Passover and Israel's departure and liberation from Egypt recorded in Exodus 12–13, Grant Macaskill demonstrates that the firsthand account and personal expression "what the Lord did for me" (Ex. 13:8) would be recited at the Passover by later generations, even though they did not live under and escape Pharaoh's tyranny. This means that participants, of whatever generation, in the Passover meal were considered participants in the historical exodus by way of their identification with the exodus generation.[2] Or as the rabbinic Passover liturgy (Haggadah) puts it, "In every generation a person is obligated to regard himself as if he had come out of Egypt."[3] So as J. Todd Billings explains, "When the Israelites remembered their deliverance from Egypt, it was not a casual act but an identity-forming one."[4]

When Jesus celebrated the Passover with his disciples on the eve of his death, he did more than self-identify with the exodus generation; he gave the meal new meaning because he was about to fulfill his mission as the true Passover Lamb and therefore liber-

---

1 See Dru Johnson, *Human Rites: The Power of Rituals, Habits, and Sacraments* (Grand Rapids, MI: Eerdmans, 2019), 99.

2 See Grant Macaskill, *Living in Union with Christ: Paul's Gospel and Christian Moral Identity* (Grand Rapids, MI: Baker Academic, 2019), 78–79.

3 "English Haggadah Text with Instructional Guide," Chabad.org, accessed May 28, 2022, https://www.chabad.org/.

4 J. Todd Billings, *Remembrance, Communion, and Hope: Rediscovering the Gospel at the Lord's Table* (Grand Rapids, MI: Eerdmans, 2018), 114.

ate his people from the tyranny of sin, death, and the devil. He was not simply commemorating the exodus with his disciples but was enacting a new exodus and a new covenant that now defines our existence in him, just as the historical exodus and old covenant defined the Israelites' existence, their identity and manner of life. And when he commanded us to eat in remembrance of him (Luke 22:19; 1 Cor. 11:24–25), he was not telling us merely to pay homage to what he did two millennia ago, just as he was not simply recalling the events of the exodus when he celebrated the Passover with his disciples.

To remember or commemorate in a biblical manner is to bring the past into the present, to allow the past to actively shape the present. And it is vital to understand that even in our remembering, God's activity is primary, preceding and motivating our own. Consider Exodus 20:24: "In every place where I cause my name to be remembered I will come to you and bless you." It is the Lord who causes us to remember him, and when we do, he is present with us and blesses us. Therefore, when we remember Christ in the Supper, we are not remembering someone who is absent and disconnected from us; we are, by faith, remembering someone who is *with us*—indeed, *in us* as we spiritually feast on him—and therefore receive all the blessings that flow from covenantal union and communion with him.[5]

Remembrance, therefore, must not be confused with reminiscence, "as if Jesus gives bread and wine only to aid our memory, our mental and emotional responses at present to things long past."[6]

---

5 See Scott Swain, "Wisdom Wednesday with Dr. Scott Swain: 'How Is Jesus Present in the Lord's Supper?,'" Reformed Theological Seminary, April 3, 2018, YouTube video, https://www.youtube.com/.

6 John C. Clark and Marcus Peter Johnson, *A Call to Christian Formation: How Theology Makes Sense of Our World* (Grand Rapids, MI: Baker Academic, 2021), 102. Cf. Marcus

The English word *remember* does not adequately capture the sense and richness of the Greek term for "remembrance" (*anamnēsis*) in both Luke 22:19 and 1 Corinthians 11:24–25.[7] Anthony Thiselton explains that to remember in the biblical sense is not simply to recall God's actions but to "assign them an active role in one's 'world.'"[8] Therefore, Thiselton argues in his comments on Paul's text that when we remember Christ and his sacrificial death in partaking of the bread and the wine, we are engaging in at least four activities. First, we are gratefully worshiping, trusting, acknowledging, and obeying our crucified and risen Lord. This is the most basic element of remembering our Lord in the meal, but our understanding of the Supper cannot be reduced to this response, as significant as it is. Second, we are participating in "the experience of *being 'there' in identification with the crucified Christ who is also 'here' in his raised presence.*" Third, we are embracing "a *self-transforming retrieval of the founding event of the personal identity of the believer (as a believer) and the corporate identity of the church (as the Christian church of God).*" Last, we are "*looking forward to the new 'possibility' for a transformed identity opened up by the eschatological consummation.*" And all this "constitutes a self-involving *proclamation of Christ's death*" that is grounded in our "identity as Christians in terms of sharing the identity of Christ."[9] Just as baptism is a rite concerned with identity, so is Communion.

A core part of participating in Communion is identifying with our crucified and risen Lord: allowing our life stories—our very

---

Peter Johnson, *One with Christ: An Evangelical Theology of Salvation* (Wheaton, IL: Crossway, 2013), 240n49.

7   Billings, *Remembrance, Communion, and Hope*, 114.

8   Anthony C. Thiselton, *The First Epistle to the Corinthians: A Commentary on the Greek Text*, NIGTC (Grand Rapids, MI: Eerdmans, 2013), 879.

9   Thiselton, *First Epistle to the Corinthians*, 880; emphasis original.

identities—to be conformed to his and anticipating the world to come, which informs who we are and how we live now.[10] This commemorative meal thus ratifies and shapes in profound ways our identity as in-Christ persons, reminding us that the structures and patterns of our lives are to conform to his. The identity that we have received in Christ by being baptized into him is maintained and developed as we feast on his flesh and blood.

This is one reason why countless Christians throughout the history of the church have insisted that only those who have been baptized in the name of the Father, Son, and Holy Spirit are admitted to the Lord's Table, to receive the sacrament of Christ's body and blood. This may seem arbitrary or even legalistic to many modern-day Christians, especially those not formed by a particular confessional heritage, but there are resolute biblical and theological—no less historical and ecclesial—reasons for such a practice.

The most profound reason why baptism must precede Communion is Christological. And this is an issue of identity. As Thomas Weinandy explains, "There is a unique theological relationship between Jesus' baptism and his sacramental enactment of the Passover Mystery within the Last Supper."[11] At his baptism in the Jordan, Jesus was declared to be the beloved Son of the Father and was empowered by the Holy Spirit for his messianic ministry. The commission—and therefore messianic identity—that Jesus received in his baptism at the Jordan was fulfilled in his crucifixion and death, his baptism at Golgotha. In his baptism into death, Jesus as the faithful and obedient Spirit-filled Son of the Father gave himself "so

---

10 See Thiselton, *First Epistle to the Corinthians*, 885–86. Cf. Tim Chester, *Truth We Can Touch: How Baptism and Communion Shape Our Lives* (Wheaton, IL: Crossway, 2020), 111–13.

11 Thomas G. Weinandy, *Jesus Becoming Jesus: A Theological Interpretation of the Synoptic Gospels* (Washington, DC: Catholic University of America Press, 2018), 316.

that those whom he would baptize in the Spirit, his Father's Spirit of Sonship, could enter into communion with his Father."[12] The historical-chronological sequence of Jesus's water baptism, death, and resurrection are therefore theologically significant. Jesus had to be baptized first in order to be commissioned and empowered for his public ministry, yes, as well as for his death and resurrection. And as persons baptized into Christ, united to him, our life pattern conforms to his. "As Jesus' baptism finds its end, its fulfillment in his death and resurrection where he comes fully into his Spirit-filled communion with his Father," Weinandy explains, "so the baptism of the faithful finds its end, its fulfillment, within the Eucharistic Liturgy wherein they come into full communion with the Father."[13] Our union with Christ (exhibited in baptism) is what makes possible our communion with Christ (exhibited in the Supper) and therefore our communion with the Father by the power of the Spirit.

And so we return to what I stated earlier about the chronology and relationship of baptism and Communion regarding identity: the identity we have received in baptism is sustained and enhanced in Communion.[14] When we are baptized into Christ, we are born again, and our very selves are reconfigured. We are not given new life in some generic sense or a burst of energy to foster who we already are but are given an entirely new existence and therefore a radically different identity in the Son. And in Communion, that identity is maintained and developed as we remember the Lord—as we identify with him, are continually transformed by him, and

12 Weinandy, *Jesus Becoming Jesus*, 316.
13 Weinandy, *Jesus Becoming Jesus*, 316–17.
14 Cf. John D. Zizioulas, *Communion and Otherness: Further Studies in Personhood and the Church*, ed. Paul McPartlan (London: T&T Clark, 2006), 80.

await the fullness of our salvation. Just as bread and wine sustain and enhance the body, so Christ's body and blood sustain and enhance our identity as in-Christ persons. As Marcus Johnson wonderfully writes, "Our mental remembrance of the significance of Christ's death is not able, and is not meant, to sustain us in our fragile and compromised states full of perplexities, doubts, tragedies, griefs, and despair that inevitably accompany us. Only Christ is able, and is meant, to do that."[15] As we remember Christ—that is, identify with him and participate in him—in this meal, our weak and vulnerable selves are maintained and elevated by him.

Like the Passover, therefore, Communion is a world-altering reality, and this holy meal reinforces with beauty and delight that "God's script for our drama does not originate from within, but in the history of Jesus Christ—his life, death, and resurrection."[16] Communion is therefore an invitation, indeed an imploring, to become more of who we already are as persons immersed into Christ and donned with his identity. It is a primary means whereby God lovingly draws us into greater fellowship with himself and thus increasingly conforms us to the image of his Son, the one in whom we have been granted sonship. As Billings states, "The true identity for the Christian is beheld and tasted at the table."[17] Communion is the sign and seal of our incorporation into and participation in Christ, and so it teaches us *whose* we are and thus *who* we are."[18]

One of the greatest lies uttered by the world today is that our true identity, our authentic self, is discovered by looking within and that we can become whoever we want to be. Conversely, the bread

---

15 Johnson, *One with Christ*, 240.
16 Billings, *Remembrance, Communion, and Hope*, 115. Cf. Brian Rosner, *How to Find Yourself: Why Looking Inward Is Not the Answer* (Wheaton, IL: Crossway, 2022), 196.
17 Billings, *Remembrance, Communion, and Hope*, 116.
18 Clark and Johnson, *Call to Christian Formation*, 103.

and wine of Communion that exhibit the body and the blood of the crucified and risen Son subvert that notion. This sacrament compels us to look to Christ alone and to use it as an aid for remembering the identity we have received in him. And remembrance is integral for continuity. If we do not remember who we are and who we are called to be in Christ, we lack continuity and therefore become dissociative—we lack proper self-consciousness. If we think one way but act another, then we subject ourselves to great confusion over who we are and what our purpose is. Remembering the Lord and who we are in him maintains and deepens our knowledge of him and ourselves. And as we remember who he is and what he has done for us, he joins us closer to himself and transforms us more into his likeness. In so doing, he maintains and strengthens the continuity between who we were born to be in baptism and who we become in communion with him—persons of the water and the blood.

Communing Beings

As an act of remembrance, understood in the biblical sense outlined above, the Supper is therefore an act of participation or communion. It is not just a symbol of our communion with Christ but is an act of feasting on the flesh and blood of our Savior and so a partaking in who he is. As the Belgic Confession states, "Just as truly as we take and hold the sacraments in our hands and eat and drink it in our mouths, by which our life is then sustained, so truly we receive into our souls, for our spiritual life, the true body and true blood of Christ, our only Savior." Though our crucified and risen Lord is seated at the right hand of the Father in the heavenly places, "he never refrains on that account to communicate himself to us through faith."[19]

19 Belgic Confession, art. 35 (*CCC* 108). Cf. Robert Bruce, *The Mystery of the Lord's Supper: Sermons on the Sacrament Preached in the Kirk of Edinburgh in A.D. 1589 by Robert Bruce*, trans. and ed. Thomas F. Torrance (London: James Clarke, 1958), 44.

That we actually feast on Christ—though in a noncorporeal manner—and so participate in his very life through such mundane elements may seem fanciful, especially to those operating under a paradigm that distinguishes sharply between the natural and supernatural, but it is none other than apostolic teaching. "The cup of blessing that we bless," Paul writes, "is it not a participation in the blood of Christ? The bread that we break, is it not a participation in the body of Christ?" (1 Cor. 10:16). The Greek word for "participation" here (*koinōnia*) is often rendered "communion," which denotes joint or mutual involvement or exchange. And such intimate fellowship with Christ himself is both represented and presented to us in the bread and wine. When speaking of "the dignity of the sacraments," John Calvin explains that baptism is the "helps and means" by which we are "ingrafted into the body of Christ," and the Supper is that which draws us "closer and closer" to Christ, "until he makes us *altogether one with himself* in the heavenly life."[20] Communion with Christ is the goal of the Christian life, meaning that all his work and teachings and precepts are directed toward that end.[21] From this we infer that we are fundamentally beings created and redeemed for communion, and this truth is evident in the accounts relaying Christ's institution of the Holy Supper.

20 John Calvin, "Mutual Consent as to the Sacraments," in *Tracts and Letters*, vol. 2, trans. Henry Beveridge (Edinburgh: Banner of Truth, 2009), 222–23; emphasis added. Cf. Calvin, *Inst.*, 4.17.1.

21 It is for this reason that the sacraments "ought to climax and crown the preached message," as Carl Henry argues. Carl F. H. Henry, *God Who Speaks and Shows: Fifteen Theses, Part Three*, vol. 4 of *God, Revelation, and Authority* (Wheaton, IL: Crossway, 1999), 479–80. When the Lord's Supper is one of two great peaks in the church's worship (the other being the preached word—an analogy I have drawn from a pastor at my church), what is reinforced is that communion or fellowship with God is the telos of the Christian life. Indeed, salvation is not just knowing about Christ but *knowing him*—personally, relationally, intimately (see John 17:3).

In the Synoptic Gospels, Jesus offers his disciples bread and wine and commands them to take, eat, drink (Matt. 26:26–28; Mark 14:22–23; Luke 22:19–20). In taking, eating, and drinking what Christ gives them, the disciples participate in Jesus's sacramental enactment because their actions are conjoined with his.[22] "Although Jesus' actions are distinct from the Apostles'," their respective actions together constitute one "sacramental act of giving and taking," Weinandy explains. "The doctrinal significance of the conjoined acts of giving and taking, the conjoined hands upon the same 'bread' and same cup, resides in Jesus bringing his Apostles into communion, literally in life-giving touch, with him."[23] Thus, by sacramentally enacting in this meal his saving death and resurrection *before* his actual death and resurrection, Jesus is revealing the telos or end goal of his death and resurrection: to bring his disciples and the church "into living communion, in living touch, with him and his sacrificial death and resurrection."[24] The very purpose of Christ's crucifixion and resurrection, signified in the bread and wine, is communion with his people. Jesus gave himself up on the cross so that he might give us himself, his life and all the benefits that flow from it.

As *signa practica* (practical signs), the bread and wine do not simply *represent* Christ's body and blood but actually *present* them to us. And as John Clark and Marcus Johnson explain, "As Christ makes himself present to the church through the Eucharist, the head of the body repeatedly and progressively *re-members* us, deepening and strengthening our union with him."[25] When we humbly

22 Weinandy, *Jesus Becoming Jesus*, 305.
23 Weinandy, *Jesus Becoming Jesus*, 306.
24 Weinandy, *Jesus Becoming Jesus*, 308. Cf. Alexander Schmemann, *The Eucharist: Sacrament of the Kingdom*, trans. Paul Kachur (Crestwood, NY: St. Vladimir's Seminary Press, 1987), 200–201.
25 Clark and Johnson, *Call to Christian Formation*, 102.

and gratefully take these signs by faith, we receive the very realities that they signify. Though Christ is not "substantially present in the Supper" because he resides physically in heaven, Calvin explains, we nevertheless experience "true and real communion" with him as we partake of this holy meal.[26] This "marvelous communion of his body and blood . . . takes place by the power of the Holy Spirit,"[27] who "is the bond by which Christ effectually unites us to himself."[28] Christ is not brought down to us, but we are raised up to him by the power of the Spirit, so that when we take and eat and drink, we receive him, and he fills our very being. As Calvin poignantly states, "By bidding us take, he indicates that *it is ours*; by bidding us eat, that it is made *one substance with us*."[29] The elements are analogous to "spiritual things" and therefore are "food for our spiritual life,"[30] enabling us to grasp Christ more firmly and "grow into one body with him."[31] Or as John Owen explains, "There is a reception of Christ as tendered in the promise of the gospel, but here [in the meal] is a peculiar way of his exhibition under outward signs, and a mysterious reception of him in them really, *so as to come to a real substantial incorporation in our souls*."[32] This does not mean that we become ontologically one with Christ in essence, as if we were somehow now divine, but that we become more unified with him relationally by participating in his life-giving humanity. Our proximity to Christ could not be greater.

---

26 John Calvin, "Second Defence of the Sacraments," in *Tracts and Letters*, vol. 2, trans. Henry Beveridge (Edinburgh: Banner of Truth, 2009), 281.

27 Calvin, *Inst.*, 4.17.26.

28 Calvin, *Inst.*, 3.1.1.

29 Calvin, *Inst.*, 4.17.3; emphasis added.

30 Calvin, *Inst.*, 4.17.3.

31 Calvin, *Inst.*, 4.17.11; cf. 4.17.2.

32 John Owen, *Sacramental Discourses*, in *Works of John Owen*, ed. William H. Goold, 24 vols. (1850–1853; repr., Edinburgh: Banner of Truth, 1966), 9:621; italics altered.

In this meal, Christ is made ours, and as he enters us and fills us, our bond and identification with him are strengthened. And the sonly identity of Christ that we have received in union with him is maintained and developed because we as sons are fortified by his crucified and resurrected self.

We may even state that, to switch metaphors and gendered language, the church's spiritual marital union with Christ is deepened. Our communion with Christ is so rich, so deep, so inexplicable that Paul likens the church's union with Christ to the union between a husband and wife. We believers are collectively the bride of Christ (2 Cor. 11:2; Eph. 5:22–23; Rev. 19:7; 21:2, 9; 22:17; cf. Ps. 45; Isa. 54:5). Christ our bridegroom has joined his people to himself by his Spirit and by the same Spirit continually gives himself to the church, his bride, in loving communion through the sacrament of his body and blood, "that we may evermore dwell in him, and he in us."[33] The new Passover meal, therefore, is an act whereby we receive our crucified and risen Lord and are invited to give ourselves to him, and in so doing preserve and deepen our oneness with him.

This language and imagery, which have both biblical and historical precedent, is no doubt startling—and that is precisely the point. To be clear, our union and communion with Christ is not sexual, but the "one flesh" union of a husband and a wife is a "profound mystery" (Eph. 5:31–32 NIV) that "refers to Christ and the church" (Eph. 5:32). Marriage pictures—and does not even capture the full substance of—the relation between Christ and his bride. Just as a husband "loves," "cherishes," "nourishes," and gives himself up for his wife, so "Christ does the church" (Eph. 5:25–29). While Ephesians 5 does not have the Eucharist in view, the sacrament

---

33 *BCP* 135.

of Christ's body and blood is a special way that he displays his gracious and extravagant love—love to the point of dying for his bride, who has been made from his side. This is shocking indeed. Not only are we loved by the Father as he loves the Son, but we are loved by Christ as a husband loves his wife. If we could fully understand the profundity and intimacy of our union and communion with Christ, then our fellowship with him would not be eternally satisfying. Indeed, may our awe for just how unfathomable our fellowship with him is never diminish but only grow.

It is important to realize that this meal is not the only way we—as persons baptized into Christ and therefore inextricably united to him by faith—commune with him. While "the Supper is an especially rich occasion for [us] to commune with Christ," Guy Waters explains, we also "commune with Christ generally . . . *by the Spirit who works by and with the Word* [Christ] and *through faith*."[34] A life characterized by faith in Christ is one of communion with him. Yet in this meal, which Christ himself marked with significance, we have, as Owen puts it, "an especial and peculiar communion with Christ," indeed, the "human nature of Christ," which is "the subject wherein mediation and redemption was wrought."[35]

While this meal is indeed an act of communion or participation, we should not dismiss the fact that it, as a sign and seal of gospel truth, is also revelatory: it is "a bond and pledge of [our] communion with [Christ], . . . as members of his mystical body."[36] And just as we are baptized into Christ and therefore ushered into

---

34 Guy Prentiss Waters, *The Lord's Supper as the Sign and Meal of the New Covenant*, SSBT (Wheaton, IL: Crossway, 2019), 103–4; emphasis original. Cf. J. I. Packer, *Taking God Seriously: Vital Things We Need to Know* (Wheaton, IL: Crossway, 2013), 161.

35 Owen, *Sacramental Discourses*, in *Works*, 9:523–24. Cf. Weinandy, *Jesus Becoming Jesus*, 307n18.

36 WCF 29.1 (*CCC* 230; emphasis added).

covenantal union with the Father by the Spirit, so we commune with the Father and the Spirit with whom Christ exists eternally in perichoretic union. By virtue of our union and communion with the Son, we are persons who exist in communion with the tripersonal God.

Not only is communion with the Trinity the sublime effect of our union and communion with Christ, the God-man and only mediator between God and man (1 Tim. 2:5), the one through whom we have access to the Father by the Spirit, but the Trinity is the very rationale for our communion. As the London Baptist Confession states, the "doctrine of the Trinity is the foundation of all our Communion with God."[37] Indeed, the doctrine of the Trinity is the very rationale for human existence and personhood. Many of us forget this reality or are ignorant of it, perhaps because we have embraced the ungodly assumption that we are insulated, lonely selves who can set the limits of our personal existence and define our own meaning and purpose in life. To adopt this lie is to misunderstand not only who we are as God's creatures but also the God in whose image we are made, who is named as a plural: "Let *us* make man in our image, after *our* likeness" (Gen. 1:26). There is one act of making, and there is one image, yet there is plurality to the name of God, who is one[38]—which we see again in the Great Commission when Jesus provides the baptismal formula "in the name of the Father and of the Son and of the Holy Spirit" (Matt. 28:19). And so the image in which we are made is "the image of the three together, the Holy Trinity."[39] Or as Hilary of Poitiers puts

---

37 London Baptist Confession, 2.3 (*CCC* 244).

38 Nonna Verna Harrison, *God's Many-Splendored Image: Theological Anthropology for Christian Formation* (Grand Rapids, MI: Baker Academic, 2010), 170.

39 Harrison, *God's Many-Splendored Image*, 170.

it, we are created in the "common image" of the divine persons,[40] who exist in eternal and ineffable communion. This means that God created us not to live autonomously but to participate in the divine reality, which is communion.

God is triune, one being existing eternally as three distinct persons in perichoretic union. Moreover, the distinctions or particularities of the three persons of the Trinity lie "in their mutual relation to one another."[41] This does not mean that God is lacking in his essence or that the three persons of the Trinity are partially divine and together constitute full deity, thus sharing in something greater than themselves. Rather, it means that the three persons— who are coeternal and coequal and who together share the same eternal perfections—are not just eternally united but also eternally interdependent in the sense that their personal particularities are given meaning in communion with one another. Put differently, each divine person's subsistence is determined in relation to the other two. For instance, the Father is properly called so because he is the source of the Son and Spirit, the one who eternally generates the Son and eternally spirates the Spirit. As Glenn Butner rightly states, "The persons are who they are in relation to one another."[42] The Trinitarian life reveals to us that personal identity is discerned and enacted only in interpersonal communion.[43]

This does not mean, however, that we can project human categories of personhood and community onto the Trinity. There

40 Hilary of Poitiers, *The Trinity*, trans. Stephen McKenna, Fathers of the Church 25 (New York: Fathers of the Church, 1954), 141 (5.9).

41 John Owen, *A Brief Declaration and Vindication of the Doctrine of the Trinity*, in *Works*, 2:406.

42 D. Glenn Butner Jr., *Trinitarian Dogmatics: Exploring the Grammar of the Christian Doctrine of God* (Grand Rapids, MI: Baker Academic, 2022), 121.

43 I am indebted to John C. Clark for this insight.

are multiple dissimilarities between the word *person* when it is used of the threefold relational subsistence of God and when it is used of humans; the three persons of the Trinity are not persons in the exact manner that we humans are persons. Three human persons are three different and therefore separate beings, but the three divine persons are not three different, separate beings. The divine essence is singular and simple, not composed of parts. Our tripersonal God is one being, and the three persons *are the being*. This means the Father, Son, and Holy Spirit do not each have a separate mind, will, and consciousness like three human persons do. Nor are the divine persons separable in their activities as human persons are. Put differently, God's actions cannot be divided between the three persons as actions can be between humans. Each person of the Trinity acts together and inseparably, though distinctly.[44] Still, with these dissimilarities noted (others could also be acknowledged, though they are peripheral to our focus here), we can safely say that we humans, who are made in the image of the tripersonal God, the one God who exists eternally in three "subsistent relations,"[45] rightly discern and enact personal identity only within a relational context.

To be truly human, to be what we are intended to be by our triune God, we must therefore exist in communion. And only when we exist in the Son, who exists eternally, inseparably, and consubstantially with the Father and the Spirit, are we truly human because we were made for communion with God. Stated differently, only when we exist in Christ—who is the "last Adam," the

44 The content in this paragraph is influenced by Butner, *Trinitarian Dogmatics*, 105–27.
45 Thomas Aquinas, *Summa Theologica*, trans. the fathers of the English Dominican Province, 5 vols. (1911; repr., Allen, TX: Christian Classics, 1981), 1.29.4, quoted in Butner, *Trinitarian Dogmatics*, 121.

true *imago Dei*, the true human being[46]—do we become who God intends us to be. As the God-man, he is not only the true revelation of God and the revelation of true humanity but also the only way to truly experiencing God and experiencing true humanity. Only by living in union and communion with him do we image God as God intends by participating in the Trinitarian communal life.[47] This does not mean that personhood is possible only for those who are in Christ or that those alienated from Christ do not image God to some extent. Indeed, all people—regardless of gender, ethnicity, social and economic status, you name it—bear the likeness of God and are unique and unrepeatable persons. But for any of us to image God in the truest sense and therefore to be human in the fullest sense, we must be joined to Christ, who "draws us, by the Spirit, into a life of faithful fellowship with the Father."[48]

Because we are created as communal, participatory beings, who we are is determined in reference to those with whom we commune and the reality in which we participate. Or as Owen puts it, we are "generally esteemed according to the company [we] keep."[49] As persons baptized into Christ, who have received the Father's Spirit

---

46 See Alan J. Torrance and Andrew B. Torrance, "Recovering the Person: The Crisis of Naturalism and the Theological Insights of Søren Kierkegaard and Karl Barth," *Crux* 48, no. 3 (2012): 55.

47 I am not suggesting, however, that the *imago Dei* is solely relational and not also functional. As beings created in God's image, we are made for communion with God and others as well as tasked to represent God and exercise dominion, as his vice-regents, in creation. For a helpful analysis of various understandings of the *imago Dei* and a helpful proposal for negotiating the tensions between both relational and functional models, see Marc Cortez, *Theological Anthropology: A Guide for the Perplexed* (London: T&T Clark, 2010), 14–40.

48 Torrance and Torrance, "Recovering the Person," 55. Cf. J. Todd Billings, *Union with Christ: Reframing Theology and Ministry for the Church* (Grand Rapids, MI: Baker Academic, 2011), 38, 48.

49 John Owen, *Communion with the Triune God*, ed. Kelly M. Kapic and Justin Taylor (Wheaton, IL: Crossway, 2007), 131.

of sonship, we keep company with the triune God. And when we recline in faith at the Communion Table, we do so "as those that are the Lord's friends," as though there is "now no difference between him and us."[50] There is no greater status than to be a person who lives in friendship and fellowship with the triune God, to be a recipient of the Father's love and grace, extended to us through the Son and by the Spirit.

Again, as in-Christ persons, we participate in his sonly existence and so are sons of the Father. To be in communion with the Father is therefore to have his love—the very love that he has for his Son—communicated to us. We have, as Owen describes it, "a comfortable persuasion and spiritual perception and sense of his love."[51] And this love assures us, who are so often vexed by anxiety and fear, of who we are: children accepted by the Father.

To commune with the Son is to exist in him and receive all the benefits he has secured for us in his redemptive-historical work. By abiding in him, we "receive *him* in all his excellencies, as he bestows *himself* upon us," as Owen puts it.[52] Christ has given us *himself*, meaning that he, by the power of the Spirit, *is personally present with us now and always*. He will never leave us nor forsake us (Deut. 31:8; Josh. 1:5; Heb. 13:5; cf. Matt. 28:20). Though others may abandon us, leaving us with a disrupted sense of self, Christ will always be present—both in us personally through the Spirit and about us through his body, the church. And because Christ has given us *himself*, he has given us *his Spirit*. We commune with Christ personally by the power of the Spirit and by the same Spirit are progressively sanctified so that we may become more like the

50 Owen, *Sacramental Discourses*, in *Works*, 9:566.
51 Owen, *Communion with the Triune God*, 113.
52 Owen, *Communion with the Triune God*, 158; emphasis added.

Son. It is an empirical fact that we become like those with whom we associate. As those who commune with Christ by the sanctifying Spirit, we cannot help but become more like the Spirit-filled Christ, who is the exact imprint of the Father's nature (Heb 1:3). Further, because Christ has given us himself and made us fully his own, we are fully accepted by the Father. While "the privileges we enjoy by Christ are great and innumerable," Owen states, the "spring and fountain whence they all arise and flow . . . is *our adoption*"—and our adoption in Christ may be described as "the grace of privilege before God."[53] As in-Christ persons, we are not tolerated by the Father but *are privileged and favored by him* because when he beholds us, he beholds us as in his Son, with whom he is well pleased (Matt. 3:17). The Father rejoices over us with gladness and exults over us with loud and joyful singing because we have been gathered to him through the work of his Son (see Zeph. 3:17–20).

And to commune with the Holy Spirit is to have him indwell us, animate us with the life of Christ, and apply to us the excellencies or benefits of Christ. Owen describes the Spirit in relation to us as the Comforter (Gk. *paraklētos*, in John 14 and 16, also commonly rendered "Helper" or "Advocate"). This does not mean that the only result of our communion with the Spirit is relief from anxiety and fear, though the Spirit certainly does alleviate such burdens. After all, when Christ was preparing his disciples for his departure and promised to send them the Spirit, he said, "Peace I leave with you; my peace I give to you. Not as the world gives do I give to you. Let not your hearts be troubled, neither let them be afraid" (John 14:27). Though he would not be with them any longer physically, he would be with them mystically through his Spirit, and they

---

53 Owen, *Communion with the Triune God*, 335; emphasis original.

therefore did not need to be fearful or anxious.[54] Yet Owen also highlights the Spirit's role of applying all Christ's promises and benefits to us. The Spirit's work entails

> bringing the promises of Christ to remembrance, glorifying him in our hearts, shedding abroad the love of God in us, witnessing with us as to our spiritual estate and condition, sealing us to the day of redemption (being the earnest of our inheritance), anointing us with privileges as to their consolation, confirming our adoption, and being present with us in our supplications.[55]

The indwelling Spirit "bears witness with our spirit that we are children of God" (Rom. 8:16) and reminds us of all that Christ has promised us, including that he would be in us and we would be in him, that he and even the Father would make their home with us (John 14:23), and that what is Christ's is ours because we are coheirs with him (Rom. 8:17).

The Spirit, our Comforter and Helper, confirms the promises of God in Christ to us, seals the benefits of Christ to us, and enables us to commune with Christ, the one through whom we have access to the Father. And one of the chief ways he does so is through the Supper. As we feast on the Father's Spirit-blessed Son, we commune with Christ by the Spirit and therefore with his Father.[56] And as we participate in the body and blood of Christ, the very humanity of our crucified and risen Lord, we, as commemorative beings, are reminded of who we are in the Son and are comforted (stemming

---

54 See John Owen, *The Holy Spirit—The Comforter*, ed. Andrew S. Ballitch, vol. 8 of *The Complete Works of John Owen*, ed. Lee Gatiss and Shawn D. Wright (Wheaton, IL: Crossway, 2023), 184.

55 Owen, *Communion with the Triune God*, 388–89.

56 On the Eucharist as communion with the triune God, see Schmemann, *Eucharist*, 167.

from the Latin *conforto*, "make stronger") by the Spirit to become more of who we are and so to live like the Son. Such knowledge casts away all anxiety over place and purpose in life, and it assuages our fear of abandonment, loneliness, and suffering. We need not worry about who we are and what we are to do or about who we are in relation to others because we know who we are in relation to our triune God.

As those who live in communion with Christ, we also live in communion with one another as in-Christ persons. To be in Christ is to be a member of his body, interconnected in Christ with all his members. The Supper is therefore "a bond and pledge" not only of our communion with Christ but also of our communion with "each other."[57] The new people that is created in baptism is symbolized and knit together more tightly in this meal. Paul explains, "The bread that we break, is it not a participation in the body of Christ?" (1 Cor. 10:16). He certainly means that we participate in the risen humanity of Christ. Yet he also means that we participate in the life of the church, which draws all its life and strength from Christ the head. Paul continues, "Because there is one bread, we who are many are one body, for we all partake of the one bread" (1 Cor. 10:17). As Geerhardus Vos comments, "The breaking of the *one* loaf of bread refers to the fellowship of the saints in the *one* body of Christ."[58] By participating in this meal, we proclaim to both ourselves and those with whom we feast that we belong to Christ and one another.

As a meal signifying our reconciliation and communion with God and one another, Communion therefore reinforces that

---

57 WCF 29.1 (*CCC* 230).

58 Geerhardus Vos, *Reformed Dogmatics: A System of Christian Theology*, single-vol. ed., trans. and ed. Richard B. Gaffin Jr. (Bellingham, WA: Lexham, 2020), 1055; emphasis original.

we cannot live truly human lives apart from vital connection to Christ and his church. God made *us* in his image as male and female (Gen. 1:26–27), and it is only in communion with one another that we as particular persons image him as he intended. Christ is the very image of God, and so to image him, to be truly human, requires that we live in communion with his body, the church, because Christ is not a solitary person but the Son who exists in eternal unity with the Father and the Spirit. Moreover, the incarnate Son of God has inextricably joined himself, the head, to the church, his body. Our triune God has deemed it fitting that the incarnate Son should not live apart from his body, the church, which means that our very experience of and communion with him is impossible without the ministry of the body. Again, no one comes to faith in the crucified and risen Lord apart from others because the faith is mediated through the church. Personal faith is not privatized faith but personal apprehension, by the power of the Spirit, of *the faith* "once for all delivered to the saints" (Jude 3).[59] Or as Macaskill poignantly states, our "very knowledge of Jesus has been brokered through the body"; thus, our remembering "the head through the ministry of the body . . . contributes to our sense of identity. It leaves no space for an individualistic account of the Christian life."[60] As persons created and redeemed for communion, we can know Christ and ourselves as in-Christ persons only when we fellowship with the church, and we cannot maintain and develop our in-Christ identity apart from the church. To be truly human, therefore, we must participate in the life of the church, our only vital connection to Christ. Thus, there is a profound difference

59 I am indebted to John C. Clark for this expression.
60 Macaskill, *Living in Union with Christ*, 82.

between a mere *social being* and an *ecclesial being*.[61] Though we are created as relational beings, we do not experience true communion by simply socializing with other people. We experience communion as God intends—that is, participation in the divine life—and therefore life abundant and true humanity when we exist *ecclesially*, participating in Christ *through the church*.

To be an ecclesial being is to be committed to the church, to participate in the life and work of the body and to live in communion with other persons united to Christ. Fundamentally, this entails making the church the primary people group with which we associate. Practically, it entails participating in corporate worship on a regular basis and being formed by the work of the church. It also involves serving the church. We cannot simply attend communal worship services, consume what is offered, and give nothing in return. Participation necessarily includes reciprocity. As we discuss in the next two chapters, to be in Christ and live like him is to sacrificially give of ourselves and our resources for the edification of others, especially other members of Christ's body. To participate in the life of our crucified and risen Lord who gives himself to us, we must give of ourselves to others. We must also accept the generosity of others. We are not self-sufficient beings, and we cannot maintain or develop our in-Christ identity apart from the self-sacrificial service of others. We enact and advance our baptismal identities when we receive from others, and we give them the opportunity to do the same by allowing them to serve us as Christ has served them. So as we, collectively, participate in the life of the church and live as ecclesial beings, communing persons, our in-Christ identity is fortified and brought closer to its fulfillment.

---

61 See John D. Zizioulas, *Being as Communion: Studies in Personhood and the Church* (Crestwood, NY: St. Vladimir's Seminary Press, 1985), 49–65.

A serious problem occurs when we as persons incorporated into Christ and his body seek to find our sense of self outside the church, and therefore outside Christ. The sacrament of Communion does not prohibit us from holding associations outside the church, but like baptism, it does teach us that the church is our primary people group. It teaches us that our fellowship with the body must regulate all other associations we have. When a man and woman bind themselves in marriage, they vow to forsake all others, meaning that their spouse is their first commitment and that all other relationships are measured by their marital union. So it is with our union and communion with Christ and his body. The world offers us endless counterfeits of the communion we were created for. Political parties, false religions, activist groups, social clubs—the list could go on—promise a sense of belonging and thus self-understanding, but they promise more than they can deliver and thus, in the end, offer us nothing at all.[62] When we locate our primary association outside Christ and his body, we experience one of two outcomes: we are either disoriented, unsure of who we are, or are profoundly deluded, confident in who we are but nevertheless operating under a false notion of self. Worldly affiliations cannot replicate or substitute what God offers us in Christ—true belonging and therefore a proper, godly sense of self.

Truth be told, there is nothing more ultimate or humane about us than our identity in Christ, which we share with all others incorporated into him. There is therefore no commonality we could share with another person or group that is more significant than the commonality we have as being in-Christ persons. Many people today struggle long and hard to form close, meaningful

62 Cf. Wolfhart Pannenberg, *Christian Spirituality* (Philadelphia: Westminster, 1983), 34.

relationships within their churches—and for many reasons—but understanding that we all share the same in-Christ identity enables us to live in joyful and loving communion with people who would otherwise be strangers and even enemies. And the sacrament of Communion reminds us of this commonality and enables us to honor and maintain it. The one loaf and shared cup subvert worldly notions of belonging and of the self by reinforcing that we are, fundamentally, participatory beings and that if we are to be truly human, to live as our triune God intends, we must exist in communion with him and his children.

Hungry and Thirsty Beings

As persons who exist in union and communion with Christ, we have therefore received all the benefits that he has secured for us through his redemptive-historical work. This truth is reinforced by the fact that Communion is a perpetual reminder of our insufficiency and therefore utter dependence on Christ. Communion signifies and seals our continuous and unending communion with Christ and therefore avails our "spiritual nourishment and growth in him," as the Westminster Confession puts it.[63] The frequency with which we partake of this sacrament and its nature as a meal give it special fortifying power. As staples for human nourishment, bread and wine by nature invigorate and satisfy us. It is no surprise, then, that our Lord would choose these elements to communicate himself to us. And just as our faith is strengthened in this sacrament, so is our very existence. The new self that we become in baptism is nourished, sustained, and enhanced when we commune with our Lord.

---

63 WCF 29.1 (*CCC* 230).

When Jesus took the bread, blessed it (or gave thanks for it), broke it, and gave it to his disciples, telling them to take and eat it (Matt. 26:26–29; Mark 14:22–25; Luke 22:14–23), he was undoubtedly performing a liturgical act that would have reminded his disciples of his multiplying the bread and fish. Although Jesus alleviated the physical hunger of thousands, he would in his death and resurrection alleviate a greater hunger, the spiritual hunger, of countless people who would be united to him by the Spirit.[64] In this meal, Jesus gives his disciples, both then and now, the Spirit-blessed bread and wine that signify his Spirit-blessed body and blood, and so he gives us *his very self* and all the benefits that flow from him.[65] Owen explains that Christ gives us "his person" because "all the benefits of his mediation arise from that fountain and spring."[66] Or as Robert Bruce poignantly remarks, "Therefore in order that the Sacrament may nourish you to everlasting life, you must get in it *your whole Saviour, the whole Christ, God and man, with all His graces and benefits*, without separation of His substance from His graces, or of the one nature from the other."[67]

And notice Christ's command: "Take, eat, . . . drink of it"—we are persons who *receive* the Lord (Matt. 26:26–27). He is the primary agent in this meal because he is the one who has accomplished our salvation and has given us himself and therefore a new identity in him—indeed, his very identity. His body was broken and given

---

64 Weinandy, *Jesus Becoming Jesus*, 301.
65 The body and blood of Christ mentioned in the institution of the Supper are synecdoches, referring not only to Christ's suffering but also to his crucified and risen humanity, which is inseparably joined—without confusion or alteration—to his divine person. Thus, we may say that in the bread and wine, Christ gives us *himself*, his crucified and risen self, not just some part of himself. Cf. Owen, *Sacramental Discourses*, in *Works*, 9:524.
66 Owen, *Sacramental Discourses*, in *Works*, 9:590.
67 Bruce, *Mystery of the Lord's Supper*, 46–47; emphasis added.

for us. His blood was shed for us, for the forgiveness of sins (Matt. 26:28). By feasting on him in our hearts with faith and thanksgiving, we receive his merits: our sinful bodies are made clean by his body, and our souls are washed by his most precious blood.[68] Thus, as we participate in this meal, we acknowledge that we are insufficient in ourselves and that Christ alone is the source of our life and salvation. We cannot, in ourselves, provide what we need most and so desperately long for—life abundant. His death and resurrection, signified in this meal, alone are the means of our salvation, the foundation of our life, the power that constitutes our Christian existence. Or as Alexander Schmemann puts it, the Eucharist "is a manifestation of man to himself, a manifestation of his essence, his place and calling in the light of the divine countenance, and therefore an act that renews and recreates him." This meal "affirms that God brought us from *nonexistence* into *being*, which means that he created us as partakers of *Being*, i.e., not just something that comes from him, but something permeated by his presence, light, wisdom, love." By receiving the bread and wine, "we recognize and confess above all the divine source and the divine calling of our life."[69]

And so Communion reinforces what we learn in baptism: we are incapable of generating our own personal identities, significance, and purpose. All of who we are is contingent on the Son sent by the Father and empowered by the Spirit. Only in him do we find true comfort and true strength, the means for living life as God intends for us. Recognizing and embracing this truth is liberating. Our modern Western world prizes independence, believing that the "authentic" person is largely self-sufficient and requires minimal input or assistance from others to live a truly meaningful life. But

68 *BCP* 135.
69 Schmemann, *Eucharist*, 185; emphasis original.

such a mindset is corrupted by godless pride. Truthfully, we are, at our very core, utterly contingent beings.

Christ himself says, "Apart from me you can do nothing" (John 15:5). And note that he says this on the heels of celebrating the Passover with his disciples, when he instituted the Supper (see John 13). His point is not that we are unable to perform basic life activities without him or even to make some generally virtuous contributions in relational separation from him—although, from a certain theological vantage point, we can fairly say that it is impossible to exist apart from him since he, as fully God, sustains all creation (see Col. 1:17). None of us, Christian or not, can continue to exist apart from the sustaining power of the one true God, in whom "we live and move and have our being" (Acts 17:28). But in this specific account in John's Gospel, Jesus is teaching us that we cannot bear fruit—that which is truly godly and spiritual, that which is characteristic of the Spirit, who is inseparable from the Son—apart from being vitally and relationally connected to the God-man. We cannot be who we ought to be and live fruitful lives as God intends without being united to our life source and having his energy continuously flowing to, in, and through us. Apart from Christ, we have no meaningful existence and shrivel up into decrepit and useless versions of what we were meant to be. But when joined to him, we take on a glorious and flourishing existence, weak though we are. The sacrament of Communion teaches us that being dependent is dignifying and beautiful. We were created not as autonomous and self-sufficient beings but as contingent persons who can live true and meaningful lives only when we feast on our Savior and draw all our comfort and strength from him alone.

But the fact that we are dependent beings who receive grace from the Lord does not mean that we are inert. Jesus commands his disciples not to passively receive but to actively take.[70] We are persons with volition and motive and thus have real agency because our wills and abilities are empowered, sanctified, and directed by the giver of life. We actively receive what Christ gives—himself and his benefits. Thus we are invited, even commanded, to grasp for Jesus and take hold of him.

We all grasp for something and seek to be satisfied by it because God created us to be hungry and then filled. The question is, What are we grasping for and consuming—both literally and figuratively—in hopes to be satisfied? Many of us are profoundly dissatisfied with our circumstances, relationships, or even ourselves. Our expectations have gone unmet, others have failed us, or we have failed ourselves. And when our dissatisfactions cause us to lose sight of who we are, we tend to look around ourselves for a remedy. Our materialistic and consumeristic world has conditioned us to believe that satisfaction and greater self-consciousness come by amassing more wealth and possessions. So we strive to accumulate certain possessions not only because we want greater fulfillment but also because we believe our wealth and belongings define who we are.[71] We are force-fed this lie by marketers and advertisers who stealthily suggest that if we only possessed certain goods and more of them, then we would be perceived a certain way and even be a certain type of person—a person with power, prestige, intimacy with others, and, of course, happiness.

The bread and wine of Communion help us crave the Lord and turn to him instead of to worldly offerings because he alone can satisfy the deepest longings of our hearts. Holding the bread,

70 Weinandy, *Jesus Becoming Jesus*, 305.
71 For a helpful discussion on consumerism and identity, see Rosner, *How to Find Yourself*, 125–42.

tasting the grain, feeling the morsel disintegrate in our mouths, smelling the vigor of the wine and feeling it warm our throats as we swallow—this ought to be a grateful meditation on the Lord's provision in Christ and an act whereby we realize with greater certainty that our existence is determined not by *what* we accumulate and consume but by *whom* we apprehend by faith.[72] Our very existence and identity are constituted, maintained, and directed by our consuming. When we consume that which is ungodly, that which is not of Christ, we are deformed into its image and thus dehumanized. But when we feed on Christ by faith, turning to him for all our resources and strength and satisfaction, we are nourished by his very life and therefore become more truly human because we take in his very humanity, which is humanity as God intends it.

The sacrament of bread and wine is therefore a perpetual reminder that we are hungry and thirsty persons who are filled and formed by what we consume. We are commended—indeed, commanded—to continually feast on Christ, not only when we partake of the bread and the cup in the context of God's people gathered for worship but throughout the week in our daily routines and activities, through prayer, meditation, Scripture reading, fellowship, and service. Many of us gluttonously consume vain and worthless fodder offered by the world and so are deformed in body and spirit. But in the sacrament of Holy Communion, we are invited to direct our appetites to Christ and to taste and see that he is good—and good *to us*. And as we partake of his Supper, we are strengthened to continually feast on him with faith throughout the week and so be satisfied by him.

72 Cf. Alexander Schmemann, *For the Life of the World: Sacraments and Orthodoxy*, 2nd ed. (Crestwood, NY: St. Vladimir's Seminary Press, 1973), 11–22.

As persons hardwired to consume and be filled, we naturally gravitate to something or someone not just for satisfaction but also for stability and assurance. Even if we believe we are largely self-sufficient and capable of attaining security through our own achievements, we intuitively recognize that security—which therefore affects how we perceive ourselves, carry ourselves before others, and live our lives—is bolstered by outside factors. And so we seek to accumulate wealth and possessions, develop and maintain relationships, and achieve a certain status to make ourselves feel secure and confident—all of which we believe form our sense of identity. But just as our accumulations and achievements cannot bring us ultimate satisfaction, neither can they bring us true security.

The bread and wine teach us to look to Christ alone for the security and assurance for which we so desperately long. Again, Christ gave himself to us for the forgiveness of sins. Forgiveness not only makes possible a relationship but also releases us from guilt and corruption, enabling us to live free from the appalling events of the past and walk forward in liberty from sin and in newness of life. The Supper is external assurance of an inward spiritual reality, that the body and blood of our crucified and risen Lord is the cause of our justification and sanctification. This meal offers us stability regarding who we are in Christ. Recall that the sacraments are sure witnesses or divine attestations of God's grace in Christ. This meal assures us that we are incorporated into Christ, the one in whom we find true life and security. He is the one through whom all things were made and by whom all things hold together (Col. 1:16–17), and he is the one who holds us together and grants us stability—not only in our circumstances but also in our self-understanding. In this meal, Christ assures us that, by his Spirit, we "share in his true body and blood as surely as our mouths receive these holy signs in his remembrance, and that all his suffering and obedience are as definitely ours *as if we personally had suffered and made satisfaction for our sins,*" as the Heidelberg Catechism puts it.[73] We may have confidence that because we are in Christ and he is in us, we are considered by the Father to be like his Son.

The fundamental aspects of who we are as persons in Christ are therefore confirmed not by subjective experiences but by an objective reality: the gospel. Assurance of self, confidence about who we are—not to be confused with pride—occurs not through self-reference but through participation in Christ, union and communion with him.[74] We humans are fragile, and even our faith is imperfect and weak, but the grace of God is sure. What he has declared to be true—that by faith we have an entirely new existence in his Son, that we are children beloved of the Father, filled with his Spirit, members of his family—is confirmed to us in Communion. All of us yearn for security, but if we look to ourselves, other sinful humans, or our circumstances for the stability we long for, despair will inevitably overtake us. Communion teaches us to shift our gaze from ourselves, our changing circumstances, and the broken world around us to the Lord alone. And this meal reinforces that our inner feelings are not ultimately authoritative. In it, we truly feast on Christ and so become more like him—provided that we receive the sacrament with faith—*even if we do not feel different after eating and drinking.* In actuality, we are raised by the Spirit to feast on our crucified and risen Lord, even if we feel distant from him.[75] We are persons who belong to the Lord and are cherished

---

73 Heidelberg Catechism, q. 79 (*CCC* 314; emphasis added).

74 See Billings, *Remembrance, Communion, and Hope*, 124–25.

75 On the dangers of a "religious feeling" that "lives and is nourished *by itself,*" see Schmemann, *Eucharist*, 143–44.

by him. Nothing and no one, not even our own failures or mistakes, can separate us from him because when Christ joins us to himself, he joins us to himself inextricably (see Rom. 8:31–39; cf. John 10:28–30).

In communing-with Christ, we are not just sustained but also enriched. His life takes ours to places we could never imagine and enhances us in ways not possible for us alone. As Vos notes, just "as bread sustains life, so wine elevates life since it makes the heart of man glad [Ps. 104:15]"; the double sign of bread and wine signify not only sustenance but also refreshment and enhancement of life.[76] In the bread and the wine of Communion, as Calvin puts it, Christ "instills life into our souls from his flesh."[77] Again, we receive not some generic burst of energy but the very life of the Son, who is preeminent in all creation, and we do so by being raised by the Spirit to where Christ resides. Christ dwells in us by the Spirit and so "raises us to himself, and transfuses the life-giving vigour of his flesh into us."[78] And it is specifically the life of the crucified *and risen* Lord that is given to us in this meal. He who defeated death in his death imparts his resurrection life, his elevating life, to us.

There is no need, then, for us to adopt self-care or self-improvement, which today so often go hand in hand, to remember who we are or to become who we think we should be. I do not mean to disregard being mindful of our own limitations and needs and then taking time to reorient ourselves so that we can be healthy physically, mentally, emotionally, and spiritually. But contemporary self-care and self-help movements assume that we have the power within

76 Vos, *Reformed Dogmatics*, 1060.
77 Calvin, *Second Defence*, 271.
78 Calvin, *Second Defence*, 279.

ourselves to restore and improve ourselves. The gospel counters that assumption, showing us that the source of our refreshment and enhancement is Christ. He beckons us, "Come to me, all who labor and are heavy laden, and I will give you rest" (Matt. 11:28). He cares for us, nourishes us, and enhances us.[79]

Yet to live in communion with God entails not only receiving from him but also giving back to him. Or in the words of Owen, it is "mutual communication": God communicates "himself unto us," and we "return unto him that which he requires and accepts."[80] Communion with the triune God is characterized by mutual activity, and the sacrament of Communion reinforces this truth in ways that have profound implications for our self-consciousness and outlook on life. When we receive Christ and his benefits in this meal, we not only commune with him and his Father by the Spirit but also gratefully give him what is rightfully his—our very selves—and so render him the honor that he deserves as Lord. This meal is an act whereby we acknowledge that we are not our own but the Lord's. While God is the primary agent in this rite, the one who presents to us his grace in Christ and so expresses to us in tangible form his goodness and love, we also act by returning love to him with gladness and gratitude, jubilantly expressing our priorities, allegiances, and affections. And so we may also call this meal an act of mutual love, from God to us and from us to God. As we participate in the divine life, we are transformed into giving beings and so become more like the God who gives.

79 For a helpful, brief assessment of self-care, see Grace Liu, "What Does the Bible Say about the Self-Care Movement?," Ethics and Religious Liberty Commission, July 5, 2019, https://erlc.com/.

80 Owen, *Communion with the Triune God*, 94.

Transformed Beings

Christ—all of who he is as the "I am" incarnate (Ex. 3:14)—is the bread of life (John 6:35),[81] and when we feast on him, he becomes part of us; indeed, he becomes "one substance with us," as Calvin puts it.[82] By communing with Christ, we descend more into him and become more like him in his Spirit-blessed humanity. This does not mean that our distinctive qualities are dissolved and that we become some strange amalgam with him. Nor does it mean that we become ontologically divine, though we do participate more deeply in the divine nature (see 2 Pet. 1:4). We are united to him yet distinct from him. He remains who he is as the crucified and risen God-man, yet we become more like him in his humanity when we feed on him by faith. And so we become authentically or fully human. He is our life (Col. 3:4), and when we eat his flesh and drink his blood, his life is transfused into us, fills us, circulates within us, and transforms us. His Spirit-blessed humanity can do nothing else because it is so potent that anyone who touches him, with faith and with his blessing, is made like him. The sick are healed, the dead are raised, lepers are made clean, the blind are given sight, demoniacs are liberated. Or think of it this way: Christ is the righteous one, and so we are righteous in him (2 Cor. 5:21). Christ is wisdom, and so we are wise in him (1 Cor. 1–2). Christ is glorious, and so we are becoming more glorious in him (2 Cor. 3:18). Those who, by faith, come into contact with the crucified and risen Christ are transformed into his image because he is the

---

81 Four times in John 6 Jesus states, "*I am* the bread of life" (or something similar to this; John 6:35, 41, 48, 51), which is one of the seven "I am" statements in John's Gospel. The "I am" statements reveal not only facets of Jesus's role and ministry but also his deity since God is revealed in the Old Testament as "I am who I am" (Ex. 3:14).

82 Calvin, *Inst.*, 4.17.3.

truly life-giving self who does not conform to who we are but rather conforms us to him who is.

Yet there is an eschatological dynamic to this sacrament that reinforces the *already* and *not yet* of who we are in Christ. In 1 Corinthians 11:26, Paul states that in participating in this meal, we "proclaim the Lord's death until he comes." This meal is a proclamation of Christ crucified and resurrected, as well as an anticipation of his return. So while the Supper connects us to the historical Jesus and reminds us of—indeed, makes us beneficiaries of—his redemptive-historical work, it is also an eschatological meal that connects us to the ascended Christ who sits in glory at the right hand of the Father and who will one day return to fully establish his kingdom (see also Matt. 26:29). This meal reminds us that while we are raised with him, we do not yet exist with him physically; we have been resurrected spiritually and so have been delivered from the dominion of sin and death in our lives, but we wait for our physical resurrection, the fullness of our adoption as sons. We partake of his crucified and risen body now, but we wait for the day when our bodies will be made like his glorified body. Thus, this meal reminds us not only that the world is not yet what it should be, and one day will be,[83] but also that we are not what we ought to be, at least not yet.[84] And as a reminder that things are not as they should be, the meal is also normative, informing us of the way things indeed ought to be.[85] It is a template of sorts for the Christian life because it represents and presents to us Christ—the last Adam, the true man, the archetype for new humanity.

83 Peter J. Leithart, "The Way Things Really Ought to Be: Eucharist, Eschatology, and Culture," *WTJ* 59, no. 2 (1997): 165–66.
84 Cf. Macaskill, *Living in Union with Christ*, 96.
85 See Leithart, "The Way Things Really Ought to Be," 166.

Like baptism, therefore, Communion makes certain demands of recipients. These historical rites of the church exhibit the church's core beliefs and practices, her ethics and mission. To be incorporated into Christ and to participate in him entails becoming more like him, in both character and behavior. Countless people today, even Christians, lack a sense of meaning and purpose as a result of not knowing who they are. For the baptized and communing person, there is no lack of meaning or purpose. We are called to be conformed to the image of Christ, who is *the true human* and *imago Dei*, and to participate in his mission. It is to these elements of Christian identity and existence that we now turn.

5

Conforming Persons

BASIC TO HUMAN EXISTENCE is the inherent feeling that we ought to progress, both as particular persons and as a collective. We all have the drive to become something more and greater. This instinct is what motivates us to form and develop relationships, advance in a career, generate wealth, cultivate a skill, and far more. We know deep within that we have a destiny, and we are hardwired to discover and fulfill it. Sadly, because so many people today, including Christians, struggle to understand their *identity*, they also struggle to understand their *purpose*, often with great frustration and hopelessness. This is because identity and purpose are inextricably linked. To understand our purpose, we must first understand our identity. This is because design shapes purpose. Tools have a specific use according to their design, and body parts have particular functions based on their unique features. Our identity is what grounds our purpose, as humans generally and as persons in Christ specifically. Yet even as identity grounds purpose, purpose reinforces and ratifies identity. Recall that our habits and behavior shape who we are and perceive ourselves to be. This means that to embody more and more our identity as in-Christ persons, we must embrace and enact the purpose we have been granted in him.

At this point, therefore, we transition from discussing primarily the *indicative truths* portrayed by the sacraments to discussing primarily the *imperative truths* portrayed by them. Put differently, we shift our primary focus from what baptism and Communion reveal about what God has *done for us* in Christ and who he says we are in his Son to what these rites *expect of us* as in-Christ persons. But even that distinction is not so neat and tidy. As we focus on our purpose in Christ, we discover even more who we are in him.

To be clear, the sacraments are first and foremost about what God has done in Christ—indeed, they present to us *Christ himself*—and therefore they are primarily Christological rather than anthropological in orientation. But we must allow the sacraments to train our imaginations to visualize and heed the imperative truths portrayed in the water, bread, and wine—and this is far different from, say, acknowledging our shortcomings throughout the week when we partake of the Supper and then pledging, often out of guilt, to do better the next week. As signs and seals of gospel truths, the sacraments exhibit both *gospel promises* and *gospel demands*. While there is a necessary ranking of the two, the indicative truths and imperative truths of the gospel go hand in hand and cannot be separated. Put differently, the indicative truths make possible the imperative truths, but the latter, though subservient to and contingent on the former, cannot be discarded. To understand the sacraments aright, we must therefore understand that they communicate to us both what God has done for us and what he expects of us. Moreover, if we want to understand properly what the sacraments reveal to us about being in-Christ persons, we must understand that they show us not only *who we are* in Christ but also *who we are called to be* and *how we are to live* in him. They proclaim to us our identity in Christ as well as our purpose in him.

A recurring theme throughout the previous two chapters is that the structure or pattern of our lives has been reconstituted by virtue of our union and communion with Christ. Who we are has been radically altered as a result of our immersion into the Son because in him we have taken on an entirely new existence and because as we commune with him, our life trajectories follow his. We have been stripped of our old self and been donned with a new self in Christ, clothed with his sonly identity, and we are called to adorn ourselves with godly apparel and so become more like him. The Father's will is that we become increasingly conformed to the image of his Son by his Spirit. This is our calling and privilege, and it is the chief imperative truth reinforced by the sacraments of baptism and Communion. This chapter therefore focuses on what it means to be conformed to Christ's image. While we cannot explore all that conformity to Christ entails, our journey here helps us discover what it generally looks like to be conformed to the true human being, the one who constitutes both our identity and purpose.

The Call to Conform

The moment we are baptized into Christ, we become adopted sons of the Father. There is no greater privilege than to be a child of God, to be a recipient of the very love the Father has for his only and eternally begotten Son and of all the benefits Christ secured for us in his redemptive-historical work. Yet there is also no greater responsibility. When a child is adopted by a human family, the child is expected to, over time, embody the family's values and so become more like the other family members. So it is for those of us adopted by the Father by virtue of our baptism into his Son. He accepts us as we are, but he does not leave us as we are.[1] The grace that God extends to us in Christ Jesus is indeed gratis, meaning that the Father freely accepts us in whatever condition we are in when we first turn to Christ in faith. Yet that same grace, applied to us by the Holy Spirit, also enables us to move beyond the wretched state we are in when we are converted to Christ. Put simply, in Christ we receive both justification and sanctification.[2]

So the moment we are immersed into the Son, we are expected to become like the Son, our elder brother, and therefore like the Father, because Christ is "the image of the invisible God" (Col. 1:15) and "the exact imprint of [the Father's] nature" (Heb. 1:3). In baptism, we are sealed with the name of the triune God, marked as his special possession and therefore called to take on the character of the same God. Indeed, the new self that we put on in baptism "is being renewed in knowledge after the image of its creator" (Col. 3:10). Our Lord wants to not only give us life but also stake a claim on our lives. If we are in Christ, then there is no leeway for us to be whoever we want to be and live however we want to live. We have renounced the world along with its ruler and have vowed to live for our triune God. We have committed our whole selves to him, and every part of who we are ought to conform to him and his will.

This offends those who have been conditioned to believe that self-fabricated "authenticity" is a supreme characteristic. We moderns suppose that to conform to someone or something else is to be inauthentic, not one's true self. The irony in this is that those of us who embrace such a teaching inevitably conform to some ideal

---

1 I heard this pithy statement, which poignantly captures the good news of Christ's work, in a personal conversation with Ben Witherington III in 2015.
2 See, e.g., Calvin, *Inst.*, 3.11.1, 6; 3.16.1.

that has captured our imaginations and affections.[3] Even marketers and advertisers who tell us to be true to ourselves usually do so by promoting something we should supposedly strive for and so conform to. And so the world that tells us to simply be ourselves speaks with a forked tongue, shouting one lie out of one side of its mouth while whispering another lie out of the other.

The truth is that conforming is natural and inevitable for humans. We are adaptable beings, and we innately conform to others. Consider what David Brooks says:

> Friends who are locked in conversation begin to replicate each other's breathing patterns. People who are told to observe a conversation begin to mimic the physiology of the people having the conversation, and the more closely they mimic the body language, the more perceptive they are about the relationship they are observing. At the deeper level of pheromones, women who are living together often share the same menstrual cycles.[4]

Not to mention that children instinctively take on the mannerisms, habits, and values of their parents. And then there is the fact that all of us want to be like someone else. We see people around us, people we know and love, or people far off from us, whom we do not know and likely will never meet, who we want to emulate in some fashion. Whether a family member, friend, mere acquaintance, celebrity, activist, scholar, you name it—there is someone

---

3   See Trevin Wax, "The Faithful Church in an Age of Expressive Individualism," *Kingdom People* (blog), The Gospel Coalition, October 22, 2018, https://www.thegospelcoalition.org/; Brian Rosner, *How to Find Yourself: Why Looking Inward Is Not the Answer* (Wheaton, IL: Crossway, 2022), 119.

4   David Brooks, *The Social Animal: The Hidden Sources of Love, Character, and Achievement* (New York: Random House, 2012), 210.

we know or know of whom we want to be like. This does not mean that all of us are necessarily dissatisfied with who we are and that we want to be completely different people, but it does reveal that we as humans are pliable and progressive. We change over time and do so as a result of what we gaze on, whom we spend time with, and what activities we participate in. We conform to some ideal that has entranced us.

The fundamental theological rationale for our impulse to conform is that we are made in God's image. To be made in the image or likeness of something or someone entails reflecting the original thing or person. We are designed to look like someone else, which means we will always conform to something or someone. God created us to look and act—indeed, *be*—like him. This knowledge is both dignifying and sobering. Hannah Anderson astutely writes,

> In God's wisdom, our identity as image bearers simultaneously elevates and humbles us. It reminds us our calling is too grand and too glorious to be contained in human categories. But it also confronts our pride by reminding us we are not God. In this sense, finding identity as image bearers centers us, putting us in our place in the best possible way.[5]

Knowing that we bear God's likeness and are called to reflect more brightly his image with each passing day reassures us of our identity and purpose. But none of us—even us Christians—image him as we ought. Only the incarnate Son of God perfectly reflects God. So if we want to know what it looks like to truly image him,

---

5 Hannah Anderson, "Reflection: Made in God's Image," in *Identity Theft: Reclaiming the Truth of Our Identity in Christ*, ed. Melissa Kruger (Deerfield, IL: The Gospel Coalition, 2018), 25.

we must look to Christ, the true *imago Dei,* and live in union and communion with him.[6] He perfectly shows us the Father because he is one with the Father (John 10:30). As he said to Philip, "Whoever has seen me has seen the Father" because "I am in the Father and the Father is in me" (John 14:9–10). Yet Christ is also the image or revelation of true humanity. He is the true, perfect human as God made man. And by virtue of his earthly life, suffering, death, resurrection, and ascension, he has become the last Adam and therefore the archetypal man, the model for new humanity. Moreover, as "the new man," Oliver O'Donovan explains, "[Christ] is the pattern to which we may [indeed, *must*] conform ourselves."[7]

Conform may seem too strong a term, implying that we lose ourselves and our own particularities as we become more like Christ. Is not *imitate* a better word, more respectful of our personal differences and perhaps even more inspiring? The language and concept of imitating Christ certainly can be helpful, and there is biblical precedent for this idea. Paul himself exhorts, "Be imitators of me, as I am of Christ" (1 Cor. 11:1; cf. 2 Thess. 3:7, 9). Yet as Michael Gorman explains, the verb here means "become," meaning that Paul is articulating a transformative process, which takes place only *in Christ* and *by the Spirit.*[8] Too often, discussions on imitation imply—likely unknowingly and unintentionally—that we follow the example of the historical Christ, who is external and at a distance. To be clear, we are certainly called to become like the

6 Cf. J. Todd Billings, *Union with Christ: Reframing Theology and Ministry for the Church* (Grand Rapids, MI: Baker Academic, 2011), 38, 48.

7 Oliver O'Donovan, *Resurrection and Moral Order: An Outline for Evangelical Ethics* (Grand Rapids, MI: Eerdmans, 1986), 146.

8 Michael J. Gorman, *Participating in Christ: Explorations in Paul's Theology and Spirituality* (Grand Rapids, MI: Baker Academic, 2019), 16.

historical Christ—for there is no other Christ than the one who entered history[9]—but as a historical figure, he is, by virtue of his immersion into our humanity and our immersion into him, also our contemporary and companion. He is present to us by his Spirit, and so we participate in him because we are in him and he is in us. Apart from participating in Christ, imitating him is impossible.

The language and concept of *conformity* captures this reality better, for to be conformed to something necessitates proximity. And indeed, Paul calls us to conformity: "For those whom he foreknew he also predestined *to be conformed to the image of his Son*, in order that he might be the firstborn among many brothers" (Rom. 8:29). The Greek adjective Paul uses (*symmorphos*) means "having a similar form, nature, or style," or "assimilated,"[10] and he wants us to understand that God predestined and called us *so that* we—all of who we are—would take on the flavor and form of Christ, our elder brother. The end goal of our calling and of the Christian life is communion with the triune God, and that communion is characterized by participation and sharing. As we commune with Christ, we share in his existence and become more like him.

Our purpose in life, therefore, is not to become authentic *in ourselves* or to express *ourselves*. To be clear, there is no denying that we are expressive beings. We express in various aspects of our lives our ideals and values and the realities larger than ourselves in which we participate. But modern secular culture has conditioned

9   This is an obvious truth that distinguishes the Son and his particular operation from that of the Father and Spirit. Whereas the Father and Spirit are involved in history, only the Son became a historical figure. See John D. Zizioulas, *Being as Communion: Studies in Personhood and the Church* (Crestwood, NY: St. Vladimir's Seminary Press, 1985), 130.

10   See BDAG 958; William D. Mounce, ed., *Mounce's Complete Expository Dictionary of Old and New Testament Words* (Grand Rapids, MI: Zondervan, 2006), 1279.

us to believe that if we wish to live satisfying and meaningful lives, then our lives should be occupied with reflecting *our* self-discovered and self-styled identities in whatever ways *we* imagine best suit *our own* particular desires and best accord with who *we* deem we are. But the gospel teaches us otherwise. Our focus is *Christ*. Our entire lives ought to be preoccupied with *him* and not ourselves because *he* is our life, and the life we now live we live by faith *in him*, the one in whom we are immersed. *He* is the content of our life and therefore the one we should conform to.

This Christological focus is reinforced by the sacrament of Communion. Paul teaches us that by eating the bread and drinking the wine, we proclaim Christ's death until he returns (1 Cor. 11:26). Yet our eucharistic proclamation is not limited to our actual eating and drinking with the gathered body. As persons who live in continual communion with the crucified and risen Lord, we are called to proclaim and show forth Christ—specifically, the *crucified* Messiah—with our entire lives. As we partake of the bread and wine, we are reminded that we are called to be eucharistic persons, persons who with humble gratitude express the goodness of Christ crucified with all of who we are in all that we do. This sacrament not only presents to us a reality larger than ourselves— namely, the gospel—but also enables us to participate in that reality. Communion—both the sacramental act and the way of life in Christ—is an expression of the greater world to which we belong. And as Christ fills us, he empowers us to manifest him and his world, the kingdom of God, in our lives and to be conformed to him and his kingdom ideals.

Thankfully, we do not need to search far and wide to understand what it means to be conformed to the image of Christ. Charles Taylor explains that "the ideal of authenticity requires that we discover and articulate our own identity."[11] Many people today have no clue as to what their authentic self is, and so they experiment in hopes of finding and articulating who they are. They try out different clothing styles and alter their physical appearance, sometimes even their physique, or they migrate from one social circle to another, and another, and yet another; they toy with different hobbies, or they flirt with various political and activist groups; some even move from job to job or experiment sexually—all this in attempts to discover their true selves. But as we have discerned, our identity as Christians—which is our primary identity and therefore the one that should regulate every feature of who we are as well as all our decisions and actions—is not something we need to unearth on our own. Our primary identity as in-Christ persons is God given, and so to be our true, authentic self, all we need to do is embody the identity we have received through baptism into Christ, who is the true, authentic human. To be truly authentic, therefore, is not to express who we perceive we are intrinsically but to express and become increasingly like the one who is extrinsic from us yet also within us. Put differently, we become our truest self when we become more like Christ.

This, of course, is much easier said than done. Thankfully, we have the sacraments—which, along with Scripture but not in place of it, testify to Christ and indeed give us Christ—to help us understand more and to equip us to become increasingly conformed to the one in whom we live in loving union and communion. As visible words of the gospel, baptism and Communion crystallize and reinforce Scripture's teaching regarding who Christ is and what he has done for us. They help us attain a firmer grasp of what it

11 Charles Taylor, *The Ethics of Authenticity* (Cambridge, MA: Harvard University Press, 1991), 81.

means to be conformed to Christ's image, and they stimulate us to that end.

Conformity in Death

The first thing we need to know about what conformity to Christ entails is that we are made like him *in his death*. Christian existence is impossible without first experiencing death, death to the old self. As those who have been baptized into Christ, we have been baptized into his death (Rom. 6:3). This is the first step in having our lives, our very selves, reconfigured in Christ. Therefore, if we want to live life like the risen Son, we must be joined to the crucified Son and die to ourselves, sin, and the world (see Gal. 2:20). This truth is pictured in baptism, which signifies, as the Westminster Confession articulates, our "giving up unto God, through Jesus Christ, to walk in newness of life."[12] Walking in newness of life, Christ's very life imparted by the Spirit, is possible only as we give ourselves up to God—that is, resign ourselves to him and deny our old, sinful selves.

We do this not at a distance from Christ but *in Christ* because we have been immersed into him, are forever joined to him, and are continually nourished in communion with him. Nor is death to self a one-off event. Sure, union with Christ in his death entails a specific, punctiliar death, but death in him is—this side of the eschaton—a continuous activity. Death in Christ is, paradoxically, *a way of life* because the Christ to whom we conform has a "cross-shaped identity."[13] Stated differently, the Christ to whom we are united and who inhabits us by his Spirit is the *crucified* Messiah.

---

12 WCF 28.1 (*CCC* 228). Cf. London Baptist Confession, 29.1 (*CCC* 284), which is, in essence, a Baptistic revision of the Westminster Confession of Faith.

13 Jason B. Hood, *Imitating God in Christ: Recapturing a Biblical Pattern* (Downers Grove, IL: IVP Academic, 2013), 75.

Yes, he is also the resurrected and ascended Messiah who infuses us with this resurrection life and power here and now. But until our bodies are conformed to (Gk. *symmorphos*) his resurrection body (Phil. 3:21) and we are therefore joined to him more fully, our lives now are primarily cross-shaped or cruciform.[14] As Søren Kierkegaard poignantly states, we are to become "contemporary" with Christ, "to know him," not only in "his loftiness" but also in "his lowliness," "his abasement."[15] We should strive to become contemporary with the whole Christ, not just the victorious Christ. In fact, as Richard Gaffin puts it, "We either have the whole Christ or we have no Christ."[16] So becoming like him necessitates participating in his humiliation, suffering, and death.[17]

This truth is explicit in the Gospels, especially in Mark's account.[18] Three times in Mark, in sequential chapters, we read that Christ identifies himself as the Messiah come to die and then states that anyone who would follow him—that is, be identified with him and participate in him, join him in his existence and mission—must die and live a life of continual death to self. In Mark 8:31–38, Jesus speaks of his approaching self-sacrifice and crucifixion, and then he calls his disciples to deny themselves and take up their own cross.

---

14 See Gorman, *Participating in Christ*, 53–76.

15 Søren Kierkegaard, *Practice in Christianity*, ed. and trans. Howard V. Hong and Edna H. Hong, vol. 20 in *Kierkegaard's Writings* (Princeton, NJ: Princeton University Press, 1991), 172.

16 Richard B. Gaffin Jr., *In the Fullness of Time: An Introduction to the Biblical Theology of Acts and Paul* (Wheaton, IL: Crossway, 2022), 396. Gaffin is commenting specifically on the inseparable gifts of justification and sanctification, but his point nevertheless applies and is related to union with Christ in both his lowliness and loftiness, which provide the grounding for not just our justification but also the twin aspects of our sanctification (mortification and vivification).

17 Consider Luther's profound notion of the "theologian of the cross" in his 1518 Heidelberg Disputation. See Martin Luther, *Career of the Reformer I*, vol. 31 of *Luther's Works*, ed. Jaroslav Pelikan, Hilton C. Oswald, and Helmut T. Lehmann (Philadelphia: Fortress, 1957), 40.

18 My attention to Mark 8–10 is informed by Hood, *Imitating God in Christ*, 74–75.

In the next chapter, Jesus again foretells his death and resurrection and then states that whoever would be first must be last, thus calling his followers to a life of self-denial and service (Mark 9:30–35). Then in Mark 10:32–34, he announces his imminent death and resurrection a third time and immediately tells his disciples that they must share in his cup of suffering and baptism into death (Mark 10:35–45). The cup and baptism that Jesus speaks of signify a life of self-denial, service, and death to self because Christ himself came not to be served but to serve and give up his life so that others might live (Mark 10:45). Carrying our cross and thereby identifying with the crucified Christ is a *daily* activity (Luke 9:23), meaning that the cross is the template for the Christian life.

Paul teaches the same. Consider Philippians 2:5–11. There Paul exhorts his listeners, including us today, to have a certain mindset, which he specifies is ours "in Christ Jesus" (Phil. 2:5)[19]—it has been given to us in union with the exalted Messiah.[20] We have this mindset because we exist in him. So we can think of Paul's statement along these lines: "Have the same thoughts among yourselves as you have in your communion with Christ Jesus."[21] And we must keep in mind that any benefit we receive in union and communion with Christ is an excellency he possesses in his very person and by

19 This verse is typically rendered in one of two ways because in the Greek the relative clause lacks a verb and one must be provided. So Paul's statement is usually translated either "Have the mindset that was in Christ" or "Have the mindset that is yours in Christ." I favor the ESV's rendering ("Have this mind among yourselves, which is yours in Christ Jesus") and find the interpretation of Bockmuehl and Gorman convincing. See Markus Bockmuehl, *The Epistle to the Philippians*, BNTC (London: A&C Black, 1997), 123–24; Gorman, *Participating in Christ*, 77–95. This rendering better captures the participatory nature of Paul's theology.

20 As Mark Seifrid explains, Paul's ordering "in Christ Jesus" instead of "in Jesus Christ," the latter of which never occurs in the New Testament, suggests an emphasis on the exalted Messiah. Mark A. Seifrid, "In Christ," in *Dictionary of Paul and His Letters*, ed. Gerald F. Hawthorne, Ralph A. Martin, and Daniel G. Reid (Downers Grove, IL: InterVarsity Press, 1993), 433.

21 BDAG 1066.

CHAPTER 5

way of his redemptive-historical activity. So the mindset that we receive *in Christ* is the very mindset *of Christ*. Paul is therefore not inviting us to remember and imitate the historical Christ who at one point *had* a specific mindset and now stands at a distance from us. No, he is imploring us to participate in the life of the historical, exalted, and present Christ, and to live according to the mindset that we have in him, which *is* his mindset because the mindset we are called to emulate "embraces both past and present" (see Phil. 2:6–11), as Markus Bockmuehl explains.[22] And this mindset is one of descent into self-emptying service and self-sacrificial death. To be sure, Christ's story also includes resurrection and exaltation. But in the larger context of Philippians 2, the mindset that we have and are called to cultivate is informed primarily by the cross, infused with resurrection power. Put differently, Paul is exhorting us—as an entire people in Christ ("Have this mind *among yourselves*," Phil. 2:5)—to conform our minds to Christ's, which means that we participate in Christ's service, suffering, and death. Self-emptying, therefore, is not antithetical to self-fulfillment but identical to it. The path to becoming our truest selves and most fulfilled selves is none other than self-denial.[23]

Our stories, our lives, our very selves should therefore follow the basic pattern of Christ's story of descent and death. He descended to us in his incarnation and so immersed himself into the reality of identification with the human condition, he descended into the waters of baptism and so immersed himself into the reality of identification with sin and sinners, and he descended into the baptism of death and so immersed himself into the reality of divine judgment

22 Bockmuehl, *Epistle to the Philippians*, 124.
23 The substance of these two sentences I gleaned in personal conversation with John C. Clark.

and condemnation[24]—all this he did so that we who have faith in him by the Spirit may be joined to him in loving and everlasting communion. And because he emerged from the grave victorious and ascended to the right hand of the Father, we are enabled to share in his sufferings and become like him in his death so that we may "know him and the power of his resurrection" and "attain the resurrection from the dead" (Phil. 3:10–11).[25]

The archetypal man therefore shows us that life in the new world order is impossible without death, specifically death to self. So if we want to be conformed to the true human, the true *imago Dei*, and live a truly human life, we as persons baptized into him must be conformed to him in his descent to death. If we want to know what our lives should look like, what our purpose is, and what bearing our choices and behavior have on our sense of identity, we must look to the cross. Gorman poignantly states, "The cross tells us something about Christ, about God, about God's Spirit's work in the world, about us, and about our benefiting from and participating in God's work that even the resurrection does not tell us."[26] But we must not assume that our focus should be on the cross per se. Rather, our focus should be on the crucified Messiah.[27] We pick up our cross and carry it, yes, but we do so with our eyes locked on Jesus.

At first glance, it may seem that this has little to no bearing for personal identity and life purpose. But nothing could be further from the truth. To be conformed to Christ in death liberates us from preoccupation with self and removes from us any confusion

24 See John C. Clark and Marcus Peter Johnson, *A Call to Christian Formation: How Theology Makes Sense of Our World* (Grand Rapids, MI: Baker Academic, 2021), 99.

25 My reading of this passage is influenced by Gorman, *Participating in Christ*, 77–95.

26 Gorman, *Participating in Christ*, 62.

27 Gorman, *Participating in Christ*, 33.

over who we are and how we should live. It also frees us from the crippling delusion that we have power within ourselves to live fulfilling lives. Modern secular culture presupposes that in order to live meaningful, purposeful, and satisfying lives, we simply need to look within our self-sufficient selves and live in whatever way most "authentically" expresses our innermost feelings. The truth is that the resources we need to live as we ought and to live truly fruitful, effective, and fulfilling lives lie not within but without. But the fact that such resources are *outside us* does not mean that they are *distant from us*. This truth is punctuated forcefully and tastefully in the sacrament of Communion. When we receive the bread and wine, we are reminded that all we need is *in Christ*, with whom we are united and who lives within us by the Spirit. And so Paul tells us that *we have* the mindset of Christ (Phil. 2:5) because we are *in Christ* (Phil. 1:1). What we need to live a truly human life is closer than we could ever imagine, even though it is external to us—that is, not originating from within us. Self-help philosophies and techniques prescribe looking within and therefore cannot secure for us true purpose and fulfillment. For true purpose and fulfillment, we must look to Christ, who is presented to us in the bread and wine as the crucified Messiah,[28] and die daily with him. Only when we lose our lives for Christ's sake do we find our lives in him (Matt. 10:39).[29]

Moreover, the call to die with Christ shows us that each of us is called "to become a little Christ. The whole purpose of becoming a

---

28 That the Supper presents Christ as the crucified Messiah is a refrain in Owen's discourses on the Supper, where he repeatedly appeals to Gal. 3:1. See John Owen, *Sacramental Discourses*, in *Works of John Owen*, ed. William H. Goold, 24 vols. (1850–1853; repr., Edinburgh: Banner of Truth, 1966), 9:517–622.

29 For an excellent discussion on losing yourself to find yourself, see Rosner, *How to Find Yourself*, 187–98.

Christian is simply nothing else."[30] Indeed, as C. S. Lewis explains, the church "exists for nothing else but to draw men *into Christ*, to make them little Christs."[31] One of the primary ways mother church nourishes her children to maturity in Christ is through the sacraments.[32] Baptism and Communion, therefore, are not just revelatory of Christian identity but also formative for Christian identity.

In baptism, we are united with the crucified and risen Son and thus are empowered by his resurrection life to die daily with him. Consider again what Martin Luther says: "A Christian life is nothing else than a daily baptism, begun once and continuing ever after."[33] Our baptism with water may be a one-time event, but our very lives as persons in Christ are lives of *baptism*, a call to descend to self-denial and self-sacrifice—so that we may know Christ more richly and intimately and be joined to him in his resurrection. And even though water baptism cannot be repeated, it can be improved, meaning applied and realized more fully. As the Westminster Larger Catechism teaches,

> The needful but much neglected duty of improving our baptism, is to be performed by us all our life long, especially in the time of temptation, and when we are present at the administration of

---

30 C. S. Lewis, *Mere Christianity* (1952; repr., New York: Touchstone, 1996), 154.

31 Lewis, *Mere Christianity*, 171; emphasis added.

32 The Reformers considered right preaching (and hearing) of Scripture and right administration of the sacraments to be the two main marks of the church (with some adding church discipline as a third mark) because these are, in the words of Robert Bruce, the "two special means" that God has chosen to "lead us to Christ." Robert Bruce, *The Mystery of the Lord's Supper: Sermons on the Sacrament Preached in the Kirk of Edinburgh in A.D. 1589 by Robert Bruce*, trans. and ed. Thomas F. Torrance (London: James Clarke, 1958), 39.

33 Martin Luther, "The Large Catechism," in *The Book of Concord: The Confessions of the Evangelical Lutheran Church*, ed. Robert Kolb and Timothy J. Wengert, trans. Charles Arand et al. (Minneapolis: Fortress, 2000), 445.

it to others; by serious and thankful consideration of the nature of it, and of the ends for which Christ instituted it, the privileges and benefits conferred and sealed thereby, and our solemn vow made therein.[34]

One way we improve our baptism is by mortifying our sinful flesh—denying our own sinful and selfish desires and looking to Christ, the truly selfless one. After all, to be baptized into Christ's death is, for us, to die *to sin*. As we apply and realize more fully our baptism into Christ by being conformed to him in his death and mortifying our sinful flesh, our identity in him is more fully realized—we become more of who we already are in him, little Christs, younger adopted sons of the Father.

We all struggle with the presence of sin in our lives, and temptation often feels overwhelming. For these reasons, mortification of sin is arduous work, and sometimes we are tempted to just give up. But understanding the relationship between mortification of the flesh and Christian identity is vital if we want to experience liberty from sin and therefore the joy and peace that come with holy living. In numerous places, Paul indicates that our identity as in-Christ persons motivates our behavior, and it is especially the rationale for rejecting sinful practices. Because we are baptized persons who are united to Christ (see Rom. 6; 1 Cor. 6), we are to flee—indeed, kill—the lusts of the flesh that try to overtake us. Knowing *who we are* and *whose we are* gives us godly motivation for fighting temptation. And when we overcome, by the power of the Spirit within us, we become more like the one to whom we are inextricably joined and therefore improve our baptism into him.

34 WLC q. 167 (*CCC* 395).

Another way we improve our baptism is by feasting on Christ and having him fill our being. As we commune with Christ, we become more like him. In the Supper, we are enabled to take on his posture of humility. We descend into death with him by submitting ourselves to the Father, giving ourselves over to his plan for our lives and receiving from his Spirit-blessed Son all the nourishment we need to live according to his will and not our own. We no longer pursue our own self-involved ambitions but resign ourselves to him, to who he has said we are in his Son and who he has called us to be in him. When we take Communion, we take on a posture of humility and submission, and we receive Christ crucified and resurrected. When we receive Christ in the Supper, we remember that we have died with him in baptism and are called to a life of continual death to self in him, just as he died to himself throughout his entire earthly life and ultimately gave himself on the cross for our behalf. We feed on the truly self-sacrificial one who came to serve and not be served so that we too may serve and give of ourselves. When we continually die to ourselves, not only in this meal but also in our day-to-day lives that are fortified by the meal, we become conformed to the image of the Son, who shows us that true humanity is marked by humility and sacrificial death to self.

Conformity in Self-Giving Love

While the cross is the template for the Christian life, death is not the end goal. Death in Christ leads to resurrection in Christ—both of which are signified and sealed in baptism—and a supreme characteristic of the new life we have received in Christ is self-giving love. So even as we die to ourselves daily by denying our sinful selves and following Christ, it is for a greater purpose: so we may give of ourselves in love as Christ has given of himself in love. Indeed, we die to ourselves *by* lovingly giving of ourselves to others. Giving of ourselves in love *is* an act of self-sacrificial death because love—true love, godly love—is not concerned with itself but rather is concerned with others. It "does not insist on its own way" (1 Cor. 13:4) but seeks to serve others, even at the cost of itself.

Just as baptism does not signify death and resurrection generically but death and resurrection *in Christ*, so the self-giving love that characterizes our new self in Christ is *Christ's love*. Consider Paul's words to the Corinthians: "For *the love of Christ* controls us, because we have concluded this: that one has died for all, therefore all have died; and he died for all, that those who live might no longer live for themselves but for him who for their sake died and was raised" (2 Cor. 5:14–15). As persons immersed into Christ and living in communion with him, we receive his love and participate in his love, which is none other than self-giving love: it enables us to live no longer for ourselves but for Christ, who died for all.

The reason Christ's love is self-giving—that is, not concerned with itself but directed toward others—is because it is divine love. Indeed, "God *is* love" (1 John 4:8). God does not possess love, as if it were some quality extrinsic to his nature or being; rather, he is love because he is triune. God is properly called love because he is tripersonal: Father, Son, and Spirit. If God were a singular, solitary person, he could not properly be called love. But God is, always has been, and always will be love because he is triune. God exists eternally as Father, Son, and Holy Spirit in loving communion, and this loving triune God is self-giving. The three divine persons give of themselves to one another as they mutually indwell one another.

This means that God's act of creation is not an attempt to find and experience love but rather an outworking of his eternal love. He "creates out of the overflow of his eternal triune love, and we were made to enjoy and respond to this very love."[35] The same is true, yet more forcefully punctuated, in God's act of redemption. And we may indeed describe this outpouring of triune love as self-giving because God wants his creatures to *know him*. The Father, Son, and Spirit—who together work in unison in creation and redemption—desire for humanity to know them in loving communion. And so God gives of himself. He creates and re-creates so that we may participate in the divine life, which is love. The Father gives the Son as mediator so that we might be reconciled to him (John 3:16), and the Son gives himself so that we might live in him and not for ourselves, to the glory of the Father. The Father gives the Spirit through the Son so that we might be drawn to the Father through the Son. And the same Spirit, who is the Spirit of both the Father and the Son, gives us the ability to live like the Son, who is the very imprint of the Father's nature. God gives himself to us so that we may know him in loving communion.

God's generous love is seen most clearly in Christ, who himself receives in order to give. He receives the Spirit from the Father in his baptism and baptizes his beloved with the same Spirit. And as the Spirit-baptized, Spirit-blessed Son of the Father, he gladly gives his sonly identity to those united to him by the Spirit of his Father. He takes what is his by rights as the one who lives in eternal communion with the Father and Spirit and gives it as grace to those joined to him by faith. So as those baptized into and communing with the Son, we are called by his Father and empowered by his Spirit to live in self-sacrificial and loving generosity. The Son gives of himself to us so that we might also give of ourselves to him and to others.

---

35 Kelly Kapic, *The God Who Gives: How the Trinity Shapes the Christian Story*, with Justin Borger (Grand Rapids, MI: Zondervan, 2018), 22.

This others-focused and others-directed way of life is precisely what characterizes the new self we have become in baptism. Indeed, it is the very self that "is being renewed in knowledge after the image of its creator" (Col. 3:10). Notice the unfinished, ongoing action that Paul speaks of: "is being renewed." The new self that emerges from the baptismal womb is not static but dynamic; it matures and grows—and it does so as it communes with Christ and continually partakes of him. Although Paul states that our new self is being renewed, indicating that we are not the primary agents in this act of renewal (see, e.g., Phil. 2:12–13), we as in-Christ persons indeed play an active role in our own renewal. Empowered by the Spirit, we are called to "put off the old self" and "put on the new self" (Col. 3:9–10). The verbs Paul uses in his exhortation here are in the middle voice, "which is often used with a reflexive sense and here designates something that we do to ourselves: we dress ourselves in Christ."[36] Simply put, we are called to become more of who we are as persons baptized into Christ and thus more of our true selves.

As Paul continues, he describes what this new self, the baptized self that has put off the body of the sinful flesh (Col. 2:11–12), looks like: it is compassionate, kind, humble, meek, patient, long-suffering, forgiving (Col. 3:12–13). Paul describes these qualities—which are manifested in relation to others—as if they were garments and then tells us to "put on love, which binds everything together in perfect harmony" (Col. 3:14). Love is the belt, as it were, that ties together the wardrobe into a cohesive outfit that expresses the new self in Christ. Therefore, to have our selves renewed after Christ's image, conformed to his very self, is to be outfitted with virtues that have others and their benefit ever in mind.

36 Grant Macaskill, *Living in Union with Christ: Paul's Gospel and Christian Moral Identity* (Grand Rapids, MI: Baker Academic, 2019), 62.

But we do not naturally want this. Born into sin, all of us are inherently selfish and self-centered. Though our old self has been put to death in Christ, buried in the watery tomb of baptism, it still emerges from time to time, like the walking dead, to wreak havoc on our lives, disrupt our communion with Christ and his body, and stunt our growth in him. And if we are honest, we are still fond of the old self and its practices, which our world cunningly yet perversely portrays as noble and virtuous. When describing the practices of the old self, Paul lists "anger, wrath, malice, slander, and obscene talk" (Col. 3:8), sins that manifest themselves within relational contexts and disrupt our communion with others—and, no doubt, our communion with Christ. Here, as in Galatians 3, Paul links our baptismal identity "with a formulaic way of speaking of unity within the variegated reality of Christian community," Grant Macaskill explains.[37] The reason we are to put off such sins is because "there is not Greek and Jew, circumcised and uncircumcised, barbarian, Scythian, slave, free; but Christ is all, and in all" (Col. 3:11). To be in Christ and filled with him means that we are united to those who are also in and filled with him.

So when we scrutinize, villainize, and ostracize others, especially those joined to us in Christ, we do not actually signal virtue or act honorably but rather act like those who are held captive to the god of this world, the "father of lies" (John 8:44) and "accuser of our brothers" (Rev. 12:10). To live in accordance with and improve our baptismal identity necessitates that we not act vengefully when we suffer wrongdoing or observe injustice. Rather than cling to our supposed "rights," we can relinquish these self-perceived entitlements for the sake of others. In doing so, we participate in Christ,

---

37 Macaskill, *Living in Union with Christ*, 62.

who did not use his divine status to his own advantage (Phil. 2:6). Put differently, to be in Christ "is to become empowered by God's very own Spirit to become like Christ by accepting rather than inflicting injustice."[38] This does not mean that we should refrain altogether from seeking justice but that our understanding of justice and methods for fostering it should take on a distinctly Christological shape. We must ever focus on and participate in the one who did not revile when he was reviled or threaten when he suffered but entrusted himself to the perfect Judge (1 Pet. 2:23).

The way of Christ is to descend to the status of a servant and give of ourselves for the benefit of others. As Luther so profoundly articulated, "I must place my faith and righteousness before God in behalf of my neighbor, cover his sins, take them onto myself, and do nothing else than act as if they are my own, just as Christ has done for us all. That is the nature of love when it is truly love."[39] True love is distinctly Christological in nature and therefore must have the well-being of others always in view. Christ rejected selfish gain in his incarnation, death, and resurrection, and as those baptized into his death and resurrection, we are called to do the same.[40]

This truth subverts modern notions of success and personal fulfillment. The world conditions us to believe that if we want to advance in life and experience true satisfaction, we must prioritize ourselves and our own interests and then pursue them without reservation—even if others pay a severe price. The gospel, however, teaches us that quality of life is determined not ultimately by our personal narratives and accomplishments but by the one

---

38 Gorman, *Participating in Christ*, 48.

39 Martin Luther, *The Freedom of a Christian: A New Translation*, trans. Robert Kolb (Wheaton, IL: Crossway, 2023), 85.

40 Gorman, *Participating in Christ*, 34.

with whom we die. We find ourselves, paradoxically, by resigning ourselves to God and giving ourselves to others. As Brian Rosner states, "The new self is modeled on the character and person of Jesus and in particular his sacrificial death on behalf of others."[41]

This truth is simple to acknowledge yet immensely difficult to embody. Thankfully, we have in the sacrament of Communion not only a reminder that we are called to participate in Christ's self-giving love but also stimulation to do the same. We receive Christ's Spirit-blessed body so that we may more fully give ourselves to others for their benefit and for the Father's glory. And as we participate in Christ's self-giving love, we take on more of his character and are conformed more closely to his person.

Conformity in Holiness

The essence of Christian living has often been captured in the adage "Love God, love others"—and rightly so, for Jesus himself summarized the Law and the Prophets using such language (Matt. 22:36–40). Love is at the core of Christian identity and the Christian life, as we have just discovered, but many people today are confused about the nature of love. As Carl Trueman states, "The concept of love has become little more than a sentiment with little or no moral shape at all."[42] We have already seen that Christian love, which is none other than Christ's love working in and through those united to him, is not a mere feeling. It necessarily expresses itself in self-sacrifice for others. Yet we need to articulate more thoroughly what participation in Christ's love looks like and how it differs radically from our world's understanding of what it means to live a life of love.

41 Rosner, *How to Find Yourself*, 195.
42 Carl R. Trueman, foreword to Luther, *Freedom of a Christian*, 13.

CHAPTER 5

Nowadays, love is understood as free acceptance—not simply as toleration of other people, no matter who they are and how they live their lives, but as affirmation and celebration of those people and their ways of life. The world today would have us believe that love is formless and lordless, free to take on whatever expression it wants without external constraints, and it does not discriminate. But Christ's love, and therefore God's love, the love that we are called to embody, is drastically different because it is characterized by holiness. The God who is love *is* holy, holy, holy (Isa. 6:3). Put differently, the God of love that we encounter in Scripture is none other than the thrice-holy God—Father, Son, and Spirit—who is wholly distinct from creation and perfect in all his ways. Therefore, to become like Christ by participating in his love means that we do not live free of external constraints. Love is not free to take on just any form or expression. That much is clear to a husband and a wife mutually committed in lifelong monogamy. No, the love of God in Christ, the very love that we participate in, is characterized by holiness.

To be clear, God *does* freely accept us as we are when we first turn to Christ in faith. But the Father does not accept us on the basis of *who we are*. He accepts us on the basis of *who his Son is and what he has done*. When we turn to his Son in faith, the Father sees us as he sees his Son—as holy, pure, righteous. To be in the Son is to be reckoned as he is. And as I stated above, even though God accepts us as we are, he does not leave us as we are. When we are made sons by being engrafted into the Son, we are expected to take on a manner of life that is consistent with his. Our lives therefore ought to take on a specific expression, one that is God given and not self-appointed.

To be donned with the identity of Christ is to receive his holy identity: adopted by the Father, we are not only *declared holy* but also *made holy* and *called to be holy*. Holiness, therefore, is not optional for the believer. And it is vital to understand that our holiness is derived from God's holiness—or better, it is a participation in God's holiness in Christ, which is not an abstract quality but an indicator of God's very identity and "a mode of God's activity."[43] Just as God *is love*, so he *is holy*. Moreover, as John Webster explains, the one God who alone is holy *is triune*, and so his holiness *is relational* because the tripersonal God is, by definition, relational. Therefore, God's holiness does not denote just his transcendence or his otherness but also and equally his imminence through condescension.[44] He is wholly other from creation, yet he separates a people from the world to share in his holy love. Webster wonderfully remarks,

> As Father, God is the one who wills and purposes from all eternity the separation of humankind as a holy people, destined for fellowship with himself. As Son, God is the one who achieves this separation of humankind by rescuing humanity from its pollution and bondage to unholiness. As Spirit, God is the one who completes or perfects that separation by sanctifying humankind and drawing it into righteous fellowship with the holy God.[45]

So when we think of God as holy, we must not imagine him as simply unlike us. Indeed, his ways are higher than our ways and his thoughts are higher than our thoughts (Isa. 55:8–9). He "dwells in unapproachable light" (1 Tim. 6:16). But this same God, "whom no one has ever seen or can see" (1 Tim. 6:16), has made himself visible in Jesus Christ, who is "the image of the invisible God"

---

43 John Webster, *Holiness* (Grand Rapids, MI: Eerdmans, 2003), 41.
44 Webster, *Holiness*, 43–45.
45 Webster, *Holiness*, 48.

(Col. 1:15). In Christ, the holy God who is wholly other has come near so that we who are broken and unholy might be made holy and whole by him and in him. God created us and re-created us out of his holy triune love so that we may participate in his loving triune holiness. So to be truly human, and therefore Christlike and godlike, is to be holy because he is holy (see Lev. 19:2; 1 Pet.1:16).

It cannot be overstated that God's triune holiness is what makes possible human holiness.[46] Specifically, it is in the Son, the one into whom we are baptized, that we are made holy—set apart from the world for fellowship with his Father by the Spirit. United to Christ, we have received the twofold grace of justification and sanctification. The Father has made us situationally holy and righteous by forgiving us of our sins and imputing Christ's righteousness to us (justification), and he is making us experientially holy and righteous by his indwelling Spirit of holiness, who enables us to put off the old self and continually put on the new self (sanctification). Because we are in Christ, the Father not only loves us with the same love that he has for his eternally and only begotten Son but also directs his holiness toward us by mortifying our sinful flesh and making us more alive in his Son by the Spirit.

This grace of holiness is signified and sealed in baptism. To be baptized into Christ is to be made holy. When we are immersed into the Son, we are separated from the world and take on a new existence in relation to the Son, in whom we are cleansed of our sin and guilt, and through whom we are reconciled to the Father by the Spirit. This means that we *are clean and holy*, like the Son, even when we do not feel that we are. When the Father declares that we are clean in his Son, we can take him at his word, for he

46 See Webster, *Holiness*, 59.

cannot lie (see Num. 23:19; Titus 1:2; Heb. 6:18). Yet the Father's declaration pertains not just to our status before him but also to what our condition ought to be. And so we are called to become increasingly holy, to become more of who we already are in the Son. And this we are able to do because Christ has baptized us with his *Holy* Spirit, who indwells us, vivifies us, and empowers us to participate in Christ's holiness.

One of Paul's objectives in reminding the Christians in Rome that they had been united to Christ in baptism was that they would live godly lives. Because they had been crucified with Christ in his death and raised to new life in him, they were to become persons characterized by righteousness rather than by impurity and lawlessness (Rom. 6). Paul's point is that baptism, though a rite administered to the believer at some time in the past, governs her life in the present and future, requiring her to live as Christ lived.[47] Paul links baptism and holiness elsewhere in his writings. In 1 Corinthians 6:11 and 10:1–5, he overtly alludes to baptism, teaching that it brings about and symbolizes a radical transformation in the life of the believer. And in the surrounding context of both passages, he calls baptized believers to live lives marked by holiness.[48] Baptized persons are therefore called to live according to the new life and identity they have received in Christ. Because we have been "washed, . . . sanctified, . . . justified in the name of the Lord Jesus Christ and by the Spirit of our God" (1 Cor. 6:11)—recall that baptism signifies and seals both justification and sanctification in Christ—we are to flee sexual immorality, idolatry, adultery,

---

47 Nicholas Taylor, *Paul on Baptism: Theology, Mission and Ministry in Context* (2016; repr., Eugene, OR: Wipf & Stock, 2017), 58–59; Taylor helpfully points to Michael J. Gorman, *Cruciformity: Paul's Narrative Spirituality of the Cross* (Grand Rapids, MI: Eerdmans, 2001), 32–35.

48 See Taylor, *Paul on Baptism*, 40–45.

homosexuality, theft, greed, drunkenness, reviling, and swindling (1 Cor. 6:9–10). Moreover, Paul says we *have been cleansed* of these sins. If these sins are practices of the old self that was drowned in baptism, we ought not try to resurrect them.

Baptism therefore subverts modern notions of human purpose and personal fulfillment. Countless people today assume that personal satisfaction is the ultimate goal in life and that if we are to experience true happiness and fulfillment, then we must be freed from external constraints. This is especially true in the realm of sexuality. Lamentably, many of us Christians have bought into this lie. We suppose that if God loves us, then he wants us to be happy and therefore permits us to pursue whatever makes us feel happy. We even think that we can use our bodies in whatever ways *we* deem permissible. We do this because we have been deceived into thinking that our bodies, like all matter, have no inherent meaning. We are the ones, we suppose, who not only generate our own identity but also give meaning to, and therefore set the moral parameters for, our physical existence.

The sacrament of bread and wine in particular confronts this lie head-on by reinforcing the truth that *matter matters*.[49] Physical objects, including our bodies, are not meaningless "stuff" onto which we can project our own personal meaning.[50] No, God grants all things meaning and purpose, and he takes certain matter and endows it with unrivaled meaning and purpose. The elements of bread and wine reveal Christ's body and blood, and his body and blood

49 I first heard the phrase "Matter matters" in my own immediate ecclesial context (likely from clergy). While it runs the risk of becoming a cliché, it articulates a truth that should be taken seriously by Christians today.

50 For a helpful, brief discussion of this reality, see Carl R. Trueman, *Strange New World: How Thinkers and Activists Redefined Identity and Sparked the Sexual Revolution* (Wheaton, IL: Crossway, 2022), 182–85.

reveal who he is, what he is like, and what he has done—he is the crucified Messiah whose body still bears his wounds. The elements of Communion therefore corroborate the truth that our bodies also reveal our persons and purpose. As Abigail Favale remarks,

> Our bodies are the visible reality through which we manifest our hidden, inner life. Each person's existence is entirely unrepeatable, and our unique personhood can only be made known to others through the frame of our embodiment. . . . Our bodies, then, serve a sacramental function, by revealing and communicating spiritual reality.[51]

Our bodies matter. They teach us that we have particular meaning and purpose, which we cannot form or manipulate at will. Our bodies also tell us that we were created for another—and specifically "another kind of body," Favale writes. "Maleness points toward femaleness, and vice versa. Our sexed body signals our inherent capacity and need for interpersonal communion."[52] All of who we are, including our body, is created for a specific purpose. And ultimately, our bodies are created for the Lord—for loving and holy communion with him. Therefore, *he* determines the meaning, purpose, and parameters of our bodily existence.

As the God of all goodness, beauty, and delight, he *does* want us to be personally fulfilled—and even experience bodily satisfaction—but the fulfillment he intends for us does not result from a life lived free from external restraint. Think of Adam and Eve: they were freest and most satisfied when they lived according to

---

51 Abigail Favale, *The Genesis of Gender: A Christian Theory* (San Francisco: Ignatius, 2022), 40.

52 Favale, *Genesis of Gender*, 41.

God's command, but the moment they transgressed his word, they were bound by sin, despair, and death.[53] What many people today assume is freedom is nothing other than servitude. In reality, we experience true freedom and fulfillment when we live according to God's good design.

As those baptized into Christ, we experience true liberty and satisfaction when we live congruously with the holy identity we have received in him. This is why Paul exhorts the Corinthians to shun sexual sins, idolatry, theft, greed, and so on (see also Col. 3:1–11). We who are joined to the Lord are "one spirit with him" (1 Cor. 6:17), and so we are to conduct our lives and use our bodies in a manner that honors, maintains, and strengthens our union with him and therefore our identity in him. We are to abandon sins not simply because they are contrary to God's law but ultimately because, as Macaskill astutely remarks, "they are contrary to our identity in Christ."[54] Conversely, to shun evil and embrace godliness is to live in accordance with our in-Christ identity and therefore to truly flourish.

Moreover, the sacrament of Communion teaches us that bodily satisfaction should accord with our union with Christ. We have been made one with him, and he gives himself to us in the meal. He satisfies us and our longings. Yet even though we are satisfied, we still get hungry. And so this meal teaches us to continually direct all our appetites—of every kind—to the Lord, who alone can satisfy all our hungers (see John 6:35). Why, then, would we want to direct our appetites and affections to avenues other than those he deems holy and profitable?

53 This insight was pointed out to me years ago, but I cannot recall who shared the observation with me. Therefore, I cannot claim this insight as my own.
54 Macaskill, *Living in Union with Christ*, 62.

It is vital to understand that we can live holy lives consistent with our baptismal identity only as we commune with Christ. We do not have the power within ourselves to be who we ought to be and, consequently, to obtain the fulfillment we so desperately long for. More specifically, we do not have the resources within ourselves to be holy as Christ is holy and therefore to be conformed to his image. Yet because we live in him and he lives in us, he enables us by his Spirit to live like him and therefore become more like him. As Gorman rightly states, Christ is "both the *paradigm* and *provider* of the rights-renouncing, others-regarding, cruciform humility and love needed for existence in the Christian community."[55] As finite, self-insufficient beings, we need something—more precisely, *someone*—from outside ourselves to enable us to lead truly worthwhile and purposeful lives. As persons baptized into Christ, we are vitally connected to him, and as persons who feast on Christ, we receive all our viability and strength from him. The sacraments, therefore, are both signs and seals of God's grace in Christ: they both reveal to us who Christ is and what it looks like to deny our sinful selves and live in accordance with the identity we have received in him, and they equip us to further conform ourselves to his loving and holy image. In particular, the sacrament of Communion sustains and enhances us week by week, fortifying us to become more like the Son into whom we are immersed. We are holy and become increasingly holy precisely because we are conjoined to Christ by faith and through our sacramental partaking of his holy body and blood.[56]

The sacraments reinforce the truth that God has reached out to us in Christ and made us his own for a specific purpose. He has

---

55 Gorman, *Participating in Christ*, 35.

56 See Thomas G. Weinandy, *Jesus Becoming Jesus: A Theological Interpretation of the Synoptic Gospels* (Washington, DC: Catholic University of America Press, 2018), 308.

adopted us in baptism and nourishes us in Communion *so that* he may have many sons by grace who are like his only Son by nature. The end goal of our election, our being chosen by God apart from any merit of our own, is that we be conformed to the image of the Son (Rom. 8:29). In baptism, the Father, who is the source of all life and love and beauty and goodness, has separated us from the world, sealed us with his Holy Spirit, and marked us as Christ's own forever.[57] In the Supper, he offers us his Spirit-blessed Son and so brings us into deeper and more intimate communion with himself by his Spirit and through his Son. And as we commune with the Father, Son, and Spirit, we are enabled by the Spirit to become more like the eternally begotten Son of the Father. The sacraments, therefore, proclaim to us with beauty and delight both who we are and who we are called to be. As visible words of the gospel, the sacraments therefore, and not ungodly images so rampant in our culture, ought to inform our purpose and morality. Baptism and Communion will not permit us to live however we want in attempts to find purpose and fulfillment. They teach us that to live a truly worthwhile and satisfying life is to live in the Son and like the Son, to be a baptized and communing person, to be a person of the water and the blood.

Yet there is even more to living life in and like the Son. As persons who are immersed into Christ and who commune with him, we are called to conform ourselves to him as well as to participate in his ministry. As persons who have been granted the identity of the Son, we therefore participate in the mission of the Son. And as we participate in the mission of the Son, we come to understand with even greater clarity who we are in him. This is the focus of our last chapter.

---

57 *BCP* 169, 189.

6

Participating Persons

COUNTLESS PEOPLE TODAY, even Christians, have no clue what
they are supposed to do in life. Sure, they have clarity on day-
to-day matters such as tending to family and domestic affairs,
going to school, working diligently at a job, contributing to
society, and so on. And many of them are certain about their
long-term goals and commitments, like advancing in a career,
saving to buy a home, exercising and eating healthy, planning
for retirement, and more. But they lack a clear sense of purpose
and calling that undergirds all their decisions and actions. They
feel bewildered when it comes to understanding their place and
purpose in life. So they busy themselves with vain activities,
perform worthwhile deeds perfunctorily without a sense of their
greater meaning, or lie inert as a result of feeling overwhelmed
by confusion.

The problem of not knowing what to do typically arises from
not having a sense of belonging. Alasdair MacIntyre puts it well:
"I can only answer the question 'What am I to do?' if I can answer the prior question 'Of what story or stories do I find myself

a part?'"[1] Other people, however, have an acute sense of purpose, but it is informed—or rather, *misinformed*—by a poor or even false story. Thus, many people today pursue activities and make commitments that will only disappoint them, lead them into despair, or deceive them even more. So it is for, say, the businessman who believes the story that amassing more power and affluence will grant him greater happiness. His goals are clear, but his achievements and expensive lifestyle do not—indeed, cannot—fulfill his longings. Nor can his charity atone for his sins. Knowing that he is not yet satisfied, he presumes that just a little more wealth will finally satiate his desires. Still haunted by guilt, he thinks that he can appease himself with just a bit more meritocratic effort. The cycle of deception and despair only continues, whether or not he realizes it. He is trapped in a story of falsehood. He does not even know what story he is in.

As persons in Christ, we know exactly what story we find ourselves a part of. We have been immersed into Christ and his story, and as people who remember him and commune with him, we ever identify with and participate in his story. What is more, the sacraments of baptism and Communion exhibit Christ's story to us week in and week out in the context of the body gathered for worship. We therefore have visual reminders of what we are to do. We discussed this in part in the previous chapter, where we discovered that conformity to Christ is integral to life in him. Our discussion focused more on the qualities or characteristics that we are to embody as persons in Christ, persons of the water and the blood, who have taken on the identity of the crucified and risen Son. This chapter shifts focus to account for specific activities and behaviors

---

1   Alasdair MacIntyre, *After Virtue: A Study in Moral Theory*, 3rd ed. (Notre Dame, IN: University of Notre Dame Press, 2007), 216.

we are called to—though we also explore more thoroughly the qualities or characteristics we ought to embody.

And so we turn our attention now to *mission*. Christian mission is often misunderstood. Many Christians these days reduce mission to overseas work or formalized church and parachurch ministry, and so mission is frequently seen as something for only a select few. To be clear, Christian mission *does* include overseas work and formalized ministry work, and that of various kinds, and not every Christian is called by God to work for gospel advancement in such contexts. But all who are in Christ are called to participate in the fundamental aspects of his mission because all Christians are little Christs. We are called to be like him and act like him, and part of acting like him is participating in his mission to the world. If we are baptized and communing persons, then we cannot evade or opt out of Christ's mission. To be baptized persons who live in communion with Christ means that the structures of our lives and our activities must and will conform to his. Moreover, as we understand more deeply and share in Christ's ministry and mission, we come to understand even more profoundly who we are in him.

We Participate in Christ's Threefold Office

We discovered in chapter 3 that Jesus is both the Spirit-baptized and Spirit-baptizing Christ. So to be baptized into Christ is to be baptized with the same Spirit that descended on him in his baptism at the Jordan. We have received the Spirit "without measure" (John 3:34) and have been given the anointing of the Spirit (1 John 2:20).[2] Something unfathomable has therefore happened: we are anointed with the same anointing that Jesus received for his role as

2 Bruce K. Waltke and Fred G. Zaspel, *How to Read and Understand the Psalms* (Wheaton, IL: Crossway, 2023), 146.

the Messiah (Gk. *Christos*).[3] As the Messiah ("anointed one"), Christ fulfills the three main offices of the old covenant that involved either liturgical or spiritual anointing: prophet, priest, and king.[4] Thus, the Heidelberg Catechism explains that Jesus was called "Christ" or "anointed" because

> he has been ordained by God the Father and has been anointed with the Holy Spirit to be our chief *prophet* and teacher who fully reveals to us the secret counsel and will of God concerning our deliverance; our only high *priest* who has delivered us by the one sacrifice of his body, and who continually intercedes for us before the Father; and our eternal *king* who governs us by his Word and Spirit, and who guards us and keeps us in the deliverance he has won for us.[5]

In fulfilling these Old Testament offices, Christ also fulfilled the calling of humanity. He is what the first Adam should have been. As Peter Leithart explains, "Jesus the last Adam fulfills the vocation of humanity. As a new man in the Spirit, Jesus is priest, conquering king, and prophet."[6] As *the Messiah*, Jesus is therefore *the true man*. And because of our incorporation into Christ, we share in his threefold office of prophet, priest, and king.[7] We are

---

3 See also John Owen, *A Discourse on the Holy Spirit as a Comforter*, in *The Holy Spirit—The Comforter*, ed. Andrew S. Ballitch, vol. 8 of *The Complete Works of John Owen*, ed. Lee Gatiss and Shawn D. Wright (Wheaton, IL: Crossway, 2023), 226–27.

4 See WCF 8.1 (*CCC* 197).

5 Heidelberg Catechism, q. 31 (*CCC* 299–300). Cf. WSC q. 23 (*CCC* 416).

6 Peter J. Leithart, *Baptism: A Guide to Life from Death* (Bellingham, WA: Lexham, 2021), 61. Cf. Jonty Rhodes, who states that the sacraments "reflect Jesus's threefold office." Jonty Rhodes, *Man of Sorrows, King of Glory: What the Humiliation and Exaltation of Jesus Mean for Us* (Wheaton, IL: Crossway, 2021), 116n1.

7 See J. Todd Billings, *Union with Christ: Reframing Theology and Ministry for the Church* (Grand Rapids, MI: Baker Academic, 2011), 160–65. This chapter is indebted to and builds on

called "Christians," the Heidelberg Catechism explains, because we are members of Christ by faith and so "share in his anointing." We are "anointed to confess his name, to present [ourselves] to him as a living sacrifice of thanks, to strive with a free conscience against sin and the devil in this life, and afterward to reign with Christ over all creation for eternity."[8]

It is vital to understand that our identity as prophets, priests, and kings "is derivative and subordinate to Jesus Christ."[9] J. Todd Billings highlights that the catechism describes Christ alone as the "*chief* prophet and teacher," our "*only* high priest," and "our *eternal* king."[10] Christ alone is the Messiah, and we *share* in his ministry. The London Baptist Confession thus explains when speaking of Christ's threefold office, "This Office of Mediator between God and Man, *is proper only to Christ*, . . . and may not be either in whole, or any part thereof transferred from him to any other."[11] Even though Christ is preeminent, he nevertheless grants us "unspeakable dignity" by "making us partakers of his anointing"[12] and conferring on us his prophetic, priestly, and kingly identity.[13]

While only select persons under the old covenant were anointed as prophets, priests, and kings, *all* who live in union and communion with Christ share in his threefold office. Just as there is neither Jew nor Greek, slave nor free, male nor female, because all are one in

Billings's excursus on the Heidelberg Catechism, Zacharias Ursinus, and our participation in Christ's threefold office. Cf. Leithart, *Baptism*, 61.

8 Heidelberg Catechism, q. 32 (*CCC* 300).

9 Billings, *Union with Christ*, 161.

10 Billings, *Union with Christ*, 161; Heidelberg Catechism, q. 32 (*CCC* 300; emphasis added).

11 London Baptist Confession, 8.9 (*CCC* 254; emphasis added).

12 Zacharias Ursinus, *The Commentary of Dr. Zacharias Ursinus on the Heidelberg Catechism*, trans. G. W. Williard (Columbus, OH: Scott and Bascom, 1851), 180.

13 Cf. Billings, *Union with Christ*, 162.

Christ, so all of us who are in Christ—regardless of our ethnicity, social status, or gender—share in the manifold ministry of the one Christ. As Peter proclaims, "You [plural] are a chosen race, a royal priesthood, a holy nation, a people for his own possession, that you may proclaim the excellencies of him who called you out of darkness into his marvelous light" (1 Pet. 2:9). Here Peter stresses all three offices—"proclaim" implies a prophetic role— and commenting on this passage, Martin Luther states, "What Christ the firstborn has in honor and dignity he shares with *all his Christians*."[14] This does not mean that all Christians are able or called to be clergy. The doctrine of the priesthood of all believers, for instance, reinforces the biblical truth that all believers have direct access to the Father through the mediatorial work of the Son and by the Holy Spirit. So the doctrine that we participate in Christ's threefold office does not preclude ecclesial order and authority. It does mean, however, that every baptized person is ordained to a general ecclesial order.

Many Christians today try to dismantle the clergy-laity distinction, thinking that it creates unwarranted hierarchy within the church. To be sure, unhealthy forms of clericalism that presuppose clergy are necessarily holier or more valuable than laypeople must be corrected. But most attempts to jettison the clergy-laity distinction misunderstand the nature of both clergy and laity, especially the latter. As John Zizioulas poignantly states, "There is no such thing as 'non-ordained' persons in the Church."[15] Baptism *is* ordination.[16]

14 Martin Luther, *The Freedom of a Christian: A New Translation*, trans. Robert Kolb (Wheaton, IL: Crossway, 2023), 50–51; emphasis added.

15 John D. Zizioulas, *Being as Communion: Studies in Personhood and the Church* (Crestwood, NY: St. Vladimir's Seminary Press, 1985), 215–16.

16 Cf. Peter J. Leithart, *Priesthood of the Plebs: A Theology of Baptism* (Eugene, OR: Wipf & Stock, 2003), chap. 3.

When we are baptized into Christ, we are transferred from the kingdom of darkness to the kingdom of light, to the new world *order*, and we are made members "of a particular '*ordo*' in the eucharistic community."[17] We receive orders to fulfill a specific task. While not all Christians are ordained to a specific ecclesial office, which requires certain qualifications and experiences, all Christians—no matter their background, pedigree, gender, social status, you name it—are ordained to the people of God by virtue of Spirit-created faith in Christ, which is a free gift granted by the Father and not based on our own merit. When we lose sight of baptism as ordination to the laity (Gk. *laos*, meaning "people" or "people assembled"), baptism is gutted of its theological, ecclesial, and missiological significance. Baptism is not just a symbol of personal faith. As we have discovered at length, baptism is far more than an expression of personal faith: it is an act from God to us whereby he seizes us as his own, makes us his sons, and brings us into new existence—with both a new status and a new purpose—in his Son.

We all share the desire to belong, and many of us aspire to belong to an elite group that has significance and impact—whether or not we realize it or are willing to admit it. By virtue of our baptism into Christ, we belong to and participate in the most outstanding and influential group of people to ever walk the face of the earth—the church. All of us who are in Christ are ordained as prophets, priests, and kings by virtue of our immersion into him, the Messiah. Put differently, as in-Christ persons, we *are* prophets, priests, and kings, and grounded in this matchless identity is our task of participating in his messianic ministry as little Christs, little anointed ones.

---

17 Zizioulas, *Being as Communion*, 216.

We Are Prophets

When Jesus baptized his church with the Spirit at Pentecost, he created a community of prophets. The prophet Joel anticipated this day, and Peter confirmed its commencement at the feast in Jerusalem:

> And in the last days it shall be, God declares,
> that I will pour out my Spirit on all flesh,
> and your sons and your daughters shall prophesy,
>   and your young men shall see visions,
>   and your old men shall dream dreams. (Acts 2:17;
>   cf. Joel 2:28)

When Joel foretold the Spirit's descent and its world-altering effects, he was speaking not of a few elite persons in a specific time but of *all people* in *the latter days*—that is, in the new world order inaugurated by Christ's death, resurrection, ascension, and sending of the Spirit. Christ pours out his Spirit on "all flesh," and the Spirit so inebriates people that they do what seems unthinkable: they prophesy, see visions, and dream dreams.[18] But this is true only for those who repent and turn to the Lord (Joel 2:13, 32). And so Peter—showing the connection between Joel's prophecy, the death and resurrection of Christ, and the outpouring of the Spirit—links repentance and baptism to the forgiveness of sins and the reception of the Spirit when the crowd asks him what they must do to be saved (Acts 2:37–38). He says, in effect, "Repent by being baptized, and you'll get the eyes of a visionary, the mind of a dreamer, the

---

18 See Leithart, *Baptism*, 93.

tongue of a prophet."[19] Regardless of our gender, age, ethnicity, or social and economic status, all of us who are baptized into Christ and with his Spirit are made prophets. But what exactly does it mean to be a prophet? And how is it that we share in Christ's prophetic ministry?

Many Christians today think a prophet is someone who foretells. After all, the Old Testament prophets predicted judgment, restoration, and key events in the life of the coming Messiah. Prophecy, therefore, is often understood as declaration about what is not yet, foretelling of future events and realities. While biblical prophets certainly predict, they do more. There is also confusion over whether prophets still exist and operate today. Since the canon of Scripture is "closed"—meaning that the Old and New Testaments are complete—many Christians believe that prophecy has ceased. The foundation of the church, which consists of apostles and prophets (Eph. 2:20), has already been laid, and it is on these two offices that the rest of the church is being built. The offices of apostles and prophets, therefore, were unique to the foundation period of the church, when the gospel first went from Jerusalem to Judea, to Samaria, and then to the ends of the earth. It is true, then, that the *offices of prophet and apostle* are unique to the early church, but that does not mean that Christians cannot perform *prophetic and apostolic work* in Christian life and ministry—that is, work that carries and proclaims the message of the ancient prophets and apostles of God throughout the world.

And so we must consider the nature of prophetic ministry. Biblical prophets do far more than simply tell what is forthcoming, and prophetic work is not limited to the unique office of prophet found

---

19 Leithart, *Baptism*, 94.

in the Old Testament and the early church. A prophet, generally speaking, is someone who speaks truth from God, about God, and on behalf of God. Prophets interpret and apply God's word to contemporary situations and hold their listeners accountable to that truth.[20] There were many prophets in the Old Testament, and a particular office of prophet existed in the New Testament, yet Jesus the Messiah is the ultimate or greatest prophet because *he is the true revelation of God*. "He is the image of the invisible God" (Col. 1:15), and he is "the way, and *the truth*, and the life" (John 14:6). None of us can understand God aright apart from Jesus Christ, the eternal Logos.

As persons immersed into Christ, who is himself *the truth* and *the prophet*, we share in his prophetic ministry. We have been anointed by his Spirit, the very Spirit that "carried along" the prophets of old (2 Pet. 1:21). As persons baptized into Christ and with the Spirit, we are endowed with the truth about Christ by "the Spirit of truth" (John 14:17; 15:26; 16:13). As little Christs and therefore little prophets, we are visionaries and dreamers; we see things the way they ought to be and are illuminated as to how we should live in light of that reality. We are also preachers; we are anointed to "confess [Christ's] name,"[21] as the Heidelberg Catechism states, *to proclaim Christ himself*. This does not mean, however, that we have the ability to be "infallible proclaimers" of truth.[22] We are not able to add to Scripture. Our prophetic message is the openly revealed and inscripturated message of

---

20 See John Owen, *A Discourse of Spiritual Gifts*, in *The Holy Spirit—The Comforter*, 290. This emphasis on application of the word (a feature I first learned in my own immediate ecclesial context from my bishop) is significant and should not be overlooked.
21 Heidelberg Catechism, q. 32 (*CCC* 300).
22 Geerhardus Vos, *Reformed Dogmatics: A System of Christian Theology*, single-vol. ed., trans. and ed. Richard B. Gaffin Jr. (Bellingham, WA: Lexham, 2020), 898.

Jesus Christ, who is truth incarnate, not some private, arcane revelation that leans in a gnostic direction. Indeed, "the *testimony of Jesus* is the spirit of prophecy" (Rev. 19:10). And this testimony of Jesus is the substance of "the faith that was once for all delivered to the saints" (Jude 3). Our prophetic message, therefore, is Christ, who he is and what he has done; the content of our preaching is the living, active, and present Christ as well as his finished, all-sufficient work and the work he continues to do through his Spirit.

And while we *share* in Christ's prophetic ministry and are filled with the same Spirit that descended on him at his baptism, he is *the superior prophet*.[23] All our prophetic ministry, therefore, is informed by and subjected to his own. We take all our cues from him, and he is the content of our message—indeed, the content of our lives. As baptized persons, we are marked as Christ's own and are anointed with his Spirit to proclaim him who has laid hold of us. This is one reason why in my own tradition the newly baptized person receives the sign of the cross with the anointing of oil on his or her forehead. As this happens, the minister prays, "Receive the sign of the Cross as a token of your new life in Christ, *in which you shall not be ashamed to confess the faith of Christ crucified*, to fight bravely under his banner against the world, the flesh, and the devil, and to continue as his faithful soldier and servant to the end of your days."[24] The primary role of a prophet is to preach, to make God and his will known to others. So to participate in Christ's prophetic ministry is to make him known, to proclaim his death and resurrection, to advertise the good news of what he has done so that others may come to faith in him and attain

23 Billings, *Union with Christ*, 162; Ursinus, *Commentary*, 177–78.
24 *BCP* 189.

maturity in him.[25] Evangelism—that is, making known the evangel, the good news of Jesus Christ—is a nonnegotiable feature of participating in Christ's prophetic ministry. If we want to be like the Son in whom we have been immersed, we must make him known by immersing others into the knowledge of who he is and what he has done.

Sharing in Christ's prophetic ministry requires that we first *know and understand* the truth, specifically the truth about Christ. Truth is not squishy and relative but definite and objective—indeed, truth is a person. We do not create our own truth based on our subjective feelings and tastes but must apprehend what is fixed and sure. This means that we are called to discern right from wrong, truth from falsehood, and wisdom from foolishness—and this we do in the Son and by the Spirit. If we are baptized into Christ and with his Spirit, forever joined to the one who is truth and indwelt by his Spirit, we cannot be indifferent toward the truth and must therefore seek to know it. So we must be persons who *learn* the truth. Jesus himself, God incarnate, a true human being, "increased in wisdom and in stature" (Luke 2:52). He who is *the truth*, who is *the teacher himself*, took on the humble posture of a student. As a boy, he desired nothing more than to dwell in his "Father's house" and know him (Luke 2:49). And so he sat "among the teachers, listening to them and asking them questions" (Luke 2:46). Even though he had great "understanding" (Luke 2:47), he did not see learning the truth of God as something beneath him. He loved the truth and sought to grow in wisdom. Because we are immersed into him, our lives should match his, and so we must take on a posture similar to his. To proclaim the truth, we must know the truth, and

25 See Ursinus, *Commentary*, 179.

to know the truth, we must learn the truth, specifically the truth of Scripture. And as we gain a firmer grasp of Scripture, we grasp more firmly *Christ himself*, the supreme subject of Scripture.

We are also called by God to *apply* that truth of Christ to our lives and current circumstances. Applying God's truth to new and current situations is characteristic of the Old Testament prophets. While they certainly foretell future events and warn of impending divine judgment, and so call people to repentance and offer them the hope of restoration, many times they interpret God's law for God's people and help them understand it in ways that fit their current contexts. Simply put, they help God's people understand what God's word recorded long ago means for them *in the now*. This is also characteristic of Christ's prophetic ministry, which is marked by giving his listeners a fresh understanding of God's law. "You have heard that it was said," he exclaims, "but I say to you" (Matt. 5:21–22, 27–28, 31–32, 33–34, 38–39, 43–44). In reinterpreting the law for them, he gives them a true understanding of it, all while showing them what it means *for them*. He, as the consubstantial Son of the Father, reveals the will of God and shows how they—and we no less today—ought to live in light of that revelation.

As persons baptized into Christ and anointed with his Spirit, we are called to participate in this aspect of his prophetic ministry. As we discovered early in our journey, the word of God is "living and active" (Heb. 4:12); it is a lively and powerful tool in the hands of the living God that accomplishes his purposes of revelation and redemption. Even though it does not directly address every issue, it gives wisdom that we may, in turn, apply to any situation in life. It does this because it presents to us *Christ himself*, who is the eternal Logos. He is, always has been, and always will be the truth. And as eternal truth incarnate, he is now and forevermore human. He knows our needs, struggles, and desires (see Heb. 4:15). So the written word that presents to us the living Word gives us wisdom for all circumstances in life, because the one to whom it testifies is our contemporary and fellow human, our elder brother who helps us navigate life in this broken and sinful world that he is now reconciling to himself (see Col. 1:20). We cannot separate Christ from his word, and so his word offers wisdom that we need to live as he would have us live, no matter the circumstances in which we find ourselves.

It should not be overlooked that we are also called to be persons who *obey* the truth. If we only know and profess the truth but fail to enact it, to be "doers of the word," then we deceive ourselves (James 1:22) and are not true prophets. A true prophet not only knows and professes the truth but also embodies the truth—otherwise, the prophetic outcry to others is shallow and duplicitous. It is nothing other than the work of a false prophet because the truth is mixed with the lie of not believing the truth. The doer of the word is, as John Calvin explains, "he who from the heart embraces God's word and testifies by his life that he really believes."[26] If we do not live according to the word of God, then it is not truly "implanted" in us (James 1:21), and our faith is dead (James 2:14–26). To be a prophet in Christ is to be overtaken by the word of Christ and transformed by it so that our lives harmonize with our knowledge and speech.

It cannot be overstated that we can participate in Christ's prophetic ministry only as we are illuminated and guided by the Holy Spirit, the Spirit of truth, who makes Christ present to us. We have

---

26 John Calvin, *Commentaries on the Epistle of Paul the Apostle to the Hebrews and on the Catholic Epistles*, trans. John Owen (Grand Rapids, MI: Baker, 1999), 296–97 (on James 1:22).

been baptized with Christ's Spirit, and we need to be continually filled and inspired by him so that we may know how to properly apply Christ's truth to our daily lives. We must also continually commune with Christ by the Spirit if we are to exercise our prophetic role effectively. We must feast continually on Christ in Scripture and be illuminated by his Spirit to grasp greater truth. And it is by the same Spirit that we are enabled to speak prophetically in our world today, to proclaim the good news of Jesus Christ and testify to his kingdom.

Our identity as prophets in Christ both exalts and humbles us. We are elevated to new heights because our lives are no longer concerned with our lowly affairs but with the Lord of the universe. We are called by Christ—who is himself the truth and therefore the one who gives meaning to and makes sense of all that is—to profess his holy name and represent him with our lives so that others may be brought into loving fellowship with him and his Father by the Spirit. We all want a voice. We want to be heard, and we want to know that what we have to say is meaningful and effective. Because we participate in Christ's prophetic ministry, we have words worth uttering and a message that is truly transformative. Our message, the gospel, cannot be silenced or bound (see 2 Tim. 2:9), and when we give our lives to learning, understanding, proclaiming, and living it, we participate in something far greater than ourselves. We testify to the one who created all things, sustains all things, and is redeeming all things (Col. 1:16–20). And so we are humbled. We are confronted with our own pride and ignorance because our identity as prophets *in Christ* reminds us that he is the ultimate prophet. He alone has "the words of eternal life" (John 6:68). As the eternal Logos, he alone knows what is ultimately true, and so we must yield to him. As we share in his prophetic ministry, our thoughts and opinions lose their luster because we come to realize with greater clarity that he alone is the truth. We lose significance in the best possible way while also being exalted in him.

We Are Priests

Many of us feel that our sins, shortcomings, and limitations prevent us from doing valuable work for the Lord. We sense that our failures and sinful tendencies limit what we can do in God's kingdom. Even as redeemed people, we are still sinful, and sin disrupts our lives. But the truth of the gospel is that those in Christ have been both justified and sanctified, called holy and righteous and made holy and righteous. By virtue of our baptism into Christ, we are holy, set apart from the world and reconciled to God. We have been saved "by the washing of regeneration and renewal of the Holy Spirit" (Titus 3:5). Baptism signifies and seals the "washing, purifying, and cleansing [of] our souls of all filth and unrighteousness."[27] It shows and promises that "as surely as water washes away the dirt from the body, so certainly his blood and his Spirit wash away my soul's impurity, that is, all my sins."[28] Moreover, the bread and wine of Communion represent Christ's broken body and shed blood, which have secured our redemption and reconciliation to the Father. In this meal, we have the sure promise that Christ our high priest has sacrificed himself for us so that we may be reunited to the Father. He has given himself for us and continues to give himself to us so that we may be at one (atonement) with his Father. As our only mediator, he has cleansed us and presents us as acceptable to the Father. Moreover, because we are holy and acceptable in him and because we have been anointed with his Holy Spirit, we now par-

27 Belgic Confession, art. 34 (*CCC* 106).
28 Heidelberg Catechism, q. 69 (*CCC* 310).

ticipate in his priestly office. We are made partakers in his holiness and share in his consecrating work.

To be a priest is to be set apart for the service of God, to be holy and to make things holy. As a "kingdom of priests," Israel was called to be a "holy nation" (Ex. 19:6), to be holy as the Lord is holy (Lev. 11:45; 19:2; 22:31–33). This calling has been extended to the church—the new people created by baptism into Christ that includes all Abraham's offspring (Gal. 3:29)—which is a "royal *priesthood*, a *holy* nation" (1 Pet. 2:9). As Leithart explains, "Jesus is the Holy One, the high priest of the new covenant. By uniting us to Jesus' baptism, our baptism announces and forms a new order of sanctity. Every baptized person is a saint, a holy person, a priest."[29] We do not need to fear or question whether we are qualified for holy work. Christ has qualified us by redeeming us, uniting us to himself, and making us partakers of his holy work. It is important to understand that we are "not merely consecrated ones," Leithart continues, "but also consecrat*ing* ones, who sanctify everything and everyone by the word of God, prayer, and thanksgiving (1 Tim. 4:4)."[30] As priests, we perform the holy work of teaching, interceding, and offering sacrifices.[31] And because all who are baptized into Christ participate in his priestly ministry, we act as priests not only in corporate worship but also, and primarily, "in our daily work, in our families, and among our friends."[32]

Therefore, the stay-at-home mom, business tycoon, administrative assistant, unmarried midlevel staffer, and janitor are just as much priests in Christ as those who occupy the clerical office

29 Leithart, *Baptism*, 67.
30 Leithart, *Baptism*, 67; emphasis original.
31 Ursinus, *Commentary*, 179.
32 Leithart, *Baptism*, 67–68.

of priest or presbyter by virtue of their ordination to the laity, the people of God, who are *the royal priesthood, the holy nation*. In no way, however, does this devalue clerical offices, to which God calls only some, or demean the significance and particularity of the work allotted to them. Clergy have a distinct and significant role in the church, the holy nation, the family of God, and are called to consecrate, lead, and serve in specific ways.[33] And it is vital to understand that those who fill particular offices in the church are charged with the task "to equip the saints [Gk. *hagiōn*, 'holy ones'] *for the work of ministry*" (Eph. 4:11–12). All the people of God, who "in one Spirit . . . were all baptized into one body" (1 Cor. 12:13), do the work of ministry, and each member is equipped by the Spirit to perform a specific kind of work (1 Cor. 12). All who are baptized into Christ, therefore, are made consecrators and share in his consecrating work of teaching, praying, and sacrificing.

In teaching others, we "show and communicate to them the knowledge of the true God."[34] One specific duty of Old Testament priests was to teach God's people the law (Lev. 10:11; Deut. 33:10; Mal. 2:7). Christ, as the true high priest, fulfilled this task perfectly in his earthly ministry and invites us, those living in union and communion with him, to participate in his teaching ministry. We get a glimpse of what this looks like in Colossians 3, a passage describing the new self that has been buried and raised with Christ in baptism. There Paul admonishes his readers, "Let the word of Christ dwell in you [plural] richly, teaching and admonishing one another in all wisdom, singing psalms and hymns and spiritual songs, with thankfulness in your hearts to God"

---

33 As Luther states, "Although we are all priests on the same level, not all can serve [in this office] or administer [the sacraments] or preach." Luther, *Freedom of a Christian*, 54–55.

34 Ursinus, *Commentary*, 179.

(Col. 3:16). As persons immersed into Christ, "in whom are hidden all the treasures of wisdom and knowledge" (Col. 2:3), we are to be filled with the word of Christ, to the point that it overflows from us to others. We are called not to speak our own opinions but to teach Christ's wisdom—indeed, *Christ himself, who is wisdom.* The church, therefore, is a school of priests who instruct one another in the way of Christ. We instill wisdom in one another so that we, as the body of Christ, may understand right from wrong, wisdom from foolishness, and godliness from ungodliness. All this is to the end that we may not be "tossed to and fro by the waves and carried about by every wind of doctrine, by human cunning, by craftiness in deceitful schemes," and may instead attain maturity, to "grow up in every way into him who is the head, into Christ" (Eph. 4:14–15). And this mutual instruction that Paul describes is part of the "putting on" of the new self that we discussed in the previous chapter. If we are to become more like Christ, we need the instruction of other persons living in union and communion with him. Likewise, our instruction assists others in putting on Christ more firmly. In doing so, we participate in mutual consecration by helping one another attain greater holiness of mind, heart, and conduct.

Our priestly teaching is not confined to the church but extends beyond it into the world. In Romans 15:16, Paul intimates that his missionary work to the Gentiles, his preaching of the gospel to them, is priestly work. As Simon Chan explains, "Bringing people to God through the proclamation of the gospel is a priestly act of offering up an acceptable sacrifice."[35] Preaching is therefore a liturgical act. This means that while the preaching of the gospel, to both

---

35 Simon Chan, *Liturgical Theology: The Church as a Worshiping Community* (Downers Grove, IL: IVP Academic, 2006), 44.

Christians and non-Christians, is a service rendered to people for their benefit, "it is first and foremost a service rendered *to God.*"[36] It is an offering to God done in the power of the sanctifying Spirit. Just as we as in-Christ persons are made holy by being baptized with the Spirit, so we offer up others to God (see Rom. 15:16) in our proclamation of the gospel by the Spirit with whom we have been baptized.[37] Put differently, we worship the Father by performing the costly work of evangelizing and discipling others with the good news of Jesus Christ so that they may be sanctified—set apart for God and made holy like him—by the Spirit.

Because we have "a correct knowledge" of God, we may "call upon" him in prayer.[38] Prayer is the lifeblood of the Christian life. Without it, we cannot commune with our triune God. And so all Christians are called to a life of prayer, to approach the living and sovereign Lord with praise, repentance, and gratitude—and it is with this posture that we are to present to him our petitions. Moreover, as priests in Christ, our mediator, we are called to intercede on behalf of others. By virtue of Christ's redemptive-historical work and our union with him, we are made worthy "to come into God's presence and intercede for others," Luther remarks. "To stand before God is the task of no one other than the priest. Therefore, Christ has made us his own so that we may spiritually enter into God's presence and intercede for another person, just as priests entered into God's presence physically and interceded for the people."[39]

---

36 Chan, *Liturgical Theology*, 44; emphasis original.
37 See John Calvin, *The Epistles of Paul the Apostle to the Romans and to the Thessalonians*, ed. David W. Torrance and Thomas F. Torrance, trans. Ross Mackenzie, CNTC 8 (1960; repr., Grand Rapids, MI: Eerdmans, 1980), 310–11 (on Rom. 15:16).
38 Ursinus, *Commentary*, 179.
39 Luther, *Freedom of a Christian*, 52–53.

Intercession is a primary function of the resurrected and ascended Christ. As our high priest, he sits at the right hand of his Father and presents us to him in prayer (Heb. 7:25). Because we have been baptized into his Son, the Father has, out of his great love and mercy toward us, "made us alive together with Christ . . . and raised us up with him and seated us with him in the heavenly places in Christ Jesus" (Eph. 2:4–6). Even though we exist physically on earth, we abide spiritually in the heavenly places *at Christ's side*. We sit next to him who is our high priest. Being in him and with him, we are therefore called to join him in his priestly activity. Thus, Paul urges us elsewhere to offer "supplications, prayers, intercessions, and thanksgivings . . . for all people" (1 Tim. 2:1). In doing so, we please our God and Savior and even share in the work of the "one mediator between God and men, the man Christ Jesus" (1 Tim. 2:3, 5).

The Father has therefore elevated us from the lowly status of a slave, who has no authority or say in family affairs, to the exalted status of a son, who shares in the dignity, honor, and power of the Father. He listens to us as he listens to his own Son. And so, as Luther provocatively states, "[The Christian's] priesthood grants him power over God, for God does what he asks and wishes."[40] This does not mean that we can manipulate God into fulfilling *our own will*. No, as Christ himself states, "Whatever you ask of the Father *in my name*, he will give it to you" (John 16:23). Our prayers must be in the name of Christ, our chief intercessor; they must take on the character of his own prayers, which are always for the sake of others and for the Father's glory. He is not a self-centered Messiah but a selfless one whose focus is ever on performing his

---

40 Luther, *Freedom of a Christian*, 53. Luther cites Ps. 145:19 for support: "He fulfills the desire of those who fear him; / he also hears their cry and saves them."

Father's will and on securing the well-being of those whom he loves. Thus John explains that "if we ask anything *according to his will* he hears us" (1 John 5:14). When we, as sons of the Father, pray in the name of Christ, the eternally and only begotten Son of the Father, and according to the will of the Father, he hears our prayers and grants them efficacy. And he does this out of his grace and paternal indulgence. As Calvin remarks, God "has made Himself our debtor not by receiving anything from us, but by graciously promising us all things."[41]

It is vital to understand that Christ's own high priestly intercession is what makes our intercessory prayers effective. Calvin explains,

> For as [prayers] gush forth from the emotion of love, in which we willingly and freely embrace one another as members of one body, so also are they related to the unity of the Head. When, therefore, those intercessions are also made in Christ's name, what else do they attest but that no one can be helped by any prayers at all save when Christ intercede?[42]

As *the high priest*, Christ is the true intercessor, and our intercession is nothing other than a participation in his own intercessory activity. We have the unfathomable privilege of being consecrators by virtue of our union and communion with Christ, the Holy One.

41 John Calvin, *The Epistle of Paul the Apostle to the Hebrews and the First and Second Epistles of St. Peter*, ed. David W. Torrance and Thomas F. Torrance, trans. William B. Johnston, CNTC 12 (Grand Rapids, MI: Eerdmans, 1963), 79 (on Heb. 6:10); translation slightly altered. In this context, Calvin is discussing God's will to reward good works and not prayer specifically, but the principle still applies since Calvin considered prayer a good work to which believers are called.
42 Calvin, *Inst.*, 3.20.19.

We who were once not a people, who were not part of the holy nation of God, are now God's people because we have received the mercy of God in Christ (1 Pet. 2:10). In Christ, we *are holy* and share in his ministry of *making others holy* through prayer. And he, as our mediator, is the one who covers the imperfections of our prayers and presents them without blemish to the Father so that they may avail.

Because we are holy in the Holy One, we also "present [ourselves] to him as a living sacrifice of thanks," as the Heidelberg Catechism states.[43] A chief role of Old Testament priests was to offer sacrifices to God for the forgiveness of sins and for expressing thanksgiving. As priests in Christ, we offer to the Father our sacrifices of praise and thanksgiving in response to Christ, who is himself the ultimate and final sacrifice for sin, "the Lamb of God, who takes away the sin of the world" (John 1:29).[44] The church, therefore, "in gratefulness for the gift of eternal life freely given and received, *offers up itself* as a holy and living sacrifice."[45] The appropriate response to Christ's offering of himself for us is to offer ourselves to him in grateful submission. And this offering of ourselves is done specially in celebration of Communion. While the Supper is most definitely not a sacrifice for the *remission of sins*—for Christ has secured that once and for all in his all-sufficient self-sacrifice on the cross—it is a sacrifice of *praise* and *thanksgiving* for what God has done in Christ.[46] In my own tradition, we pray, "We offer and present to you, O Lord, ourselves, our souls and bodies, to be a

---

43 Heidelberg Catechism, q. 32 (*CCC* 300).

44 Cf. Billings, *Union with Christ*, 164.

45 Chan, *Liturgical Theology*, 77.

46 For a classic Protestant affirmation of this distinction, see, e.g., Calvin, *Inst.*, 4.17.44; 4.18.10, 13, 17; Philipp Melanchthon, *The Chief Theological Topics: Loci Praecipui Theologici, 1559*, 2nd Eng. ed., trans. J. A. O. Preus (St. Louis, MO: Concordia, 2011), 280–81, 283.

reasonable, holy, and living sacrifice."[47] In this meal, therefore, we are transformed more into the likeness of the one who gave himself for us. As we receive him in Communion, we are enabled by his Spirit to function as little priests who offer ourselves up to God for his service throughout the week.

Our priestly sacrifice entails many things, and chief among them is the grateful praise to the Father for what he has done for us in Christ and by his Spirit. Yet there are other important features that are helpful to consider here—which, no doubt, are ways for us to glorify God.

In Romans 12:1, we find a classic call to offer sacrifice to God. Paul exhorts those of us baptized into Christ (Rom. 6:4–6) to "present [our] bodies as a living sacrifice, holy and acceptable to God" (Rom. 12:1). It is significant that Paul mentions our *bodies* here—though, of course, he has our whole selves in view because in Romans 12:2 he addresses our "mind." Earlier in the letter, he exhorts us to present ourselves and our "members" (that is, our bodies) "to God as instruments for righteousness" (Rom. 6:13). This act of presenting ourselves along with our bodies in worship to God denotes priestly activity (cf. 1 Pet. 2:5). And priestly work is physical work. Priests use their bodies in specific and often taxing ways. Priestly work is embodied work that requires focus, discipline, and self-control. So when Paul urges us to present our bodies as living sacrifices, he is calling us to commit all of who we are in our bodily existence to the Lord and to his service.

As we discovered in the previous chapter, our bodies have specific meaning, and we are not the ones who determine the parameters for our physical existence. Only our Creator and Redeemer can

---

47 *BCP* 117.

do that. So when Paul exhorts us to present our bodies as a living sacrifice that is "holy and acceptable to God," he is exhorting us to use our bodies in a priestly manner for God's service, not for self-gratification and self-exploitation (Rom. 12:1). Our bodies belong to the Lord, just as Christ's did. He used his body not for selfish gain but for the sake of God and others. Moreover, if we are to use our bodies in a manner that is holy and acceptable to God, we must not be "conformed to this world" (Rom. 12:2). We must be set apart from the world, which today is frightfully confused over what the human body is for and how it can be "used" and "treated," as if it were some appendage to our true selves. And this confusion has unfathomable ramifications for personal identity. If we think our bodies can be used however we want and to whatever end we want, then we ourselves amount to nothing more than selfish in-dividuals who have no meaning outside ourselves. If we think our bodies are pliable objects that can be manipulated at will to suit our own particular interests and tastes, then we ourselves amount to nothing more than meaningless stuff. We cheapen ourselves and others with such a mindset. We have no dignity and no purpose, and others cannot confirm dignity or purpose for us since they too are most likely concerned with only themselves.

But the gospel, and specifically the sacraments of the gospel, teach us otherwise. Bodily existence matters. And both baptism and Communion have their ultimate grounding in the incarnation, God the Son's becoming man.[48] Because he took on human flesh, our flesh has renewed dignity and purpose. It has meaning—and meaning far greater than what the world could ever ascribe to it.

---

48 For an excellent discussion of the sacraments being grounded in the incarnation, see John C. Clark and Marcus Peter Johnson, *The Incarnation of God: The Mystery of the Gospel as the Foundation of Evangelical Theology* (Wheaton, IL: Crossway, 2015), 189–205.

Therefore, if we are to partake in Christ's priestly ministry and have a holy self-consciousness as priests in him, we cannot tolerate or affirm the world's unholy views of the human body. Rather, we must attain a godly understanding of what the body is, what and whom it is made for, and how it should therefore be directed. And in the context of Romans 12, Paul explains that the telos of the human body is the glory of God and the benefit of others because its origin is the self-giving, others-focused God of all creation. To use our bodies as "members of righteousness" in a manner that is "holy and acceptable to God" is a primary way we enact the baptismal identities we have received in Christ, our great high priest and Passover Lamb, who sacrificed his own body for the life of the world.

As we discovered in the previous chapter, Christ's self-sacrificial service is always on behalf of others, and it is that same service to which we are called as persons who participate in his priestly ministry. In Romans 12, Paul teaches us that integral to self-sacrifice is not being conformed to the pattern of this world and instead being transformed by the renewal of our minds. In doing so, we "discern what is the will of God, what is good and acceptable and perfect" (Rom. 12:2). In the remainder of the chapter, Paul details what the will of God is for those baptized into Christ—what it looks like to live as those united to him in his death and resurrection (Rom. 6:4)—and therefore what presenting ourselves as living sacrifices entails. He explains that to live in service of God is to live in service of others. Put differently, we lay our lives down for others, to the glory of God, so that we might build them up. And the gifts that we have been given in Christ are to be used specifically for edifying Christ's body (cf. 1 Cor. 12). Assuming a posture of humility, serving one another, and trusting in the Lord to do his work on our behalf are all ways in which we offer ourselves as living sacrifices to God.

When we self-sacrificially serve others, we heed, even if only in small ways, the words of Christ himself, our high priest, who is himself both the sacrificer and the sacrifice: "Greater love has no one than this, that someone lay down his life for his friends" (John 15:13).[49] Christ did this for us, and he calls us to lay down our lives for one another in service, even to the point of stooping to wash one another's feet, to consecrate their steps, their walk in life (John 13:1–20). It is no minor detail that Jesus did this in the context of the Passover, when he instituted the sacrament of Communion. As we abide in Christ and commune with him, drawing all our life and strength from him as a branch does from the vine, we are enabled to lay down our lives for one another (John 15:1–17). As Chan remarks, "Communion in the body of Christ is no less than loving to the point of death, just as Christ himself, in love, humbled himself and became obedient even to death (cf. Phil. 2:8)."[50] When we receive Communion in the context of the body gathered for worship, we are confronted with our identity and calling as persons baptized into Christ's death and resurrection: we are persons who pour ourselves out like a drink offering so that others may abound in Christ (see Phil. 2:17). As priests, therefore, our entire bodily existence is aimed at serving God and others through teaching, praying, and offering sacrifices. When we do, we become more like *the priest* in whom we are immersed and with whom we commune.

We Are Kings

We have discovered variously in our journey that we as persons baptized into Christ have been not only buried with him but also

49 This paragraph is informed by Chan, *Liturgical Theology*, 78.
50 Chan, *Liturgical Theology*, 78.

raised with him. In Romans 6, we learn that we have been raised from death to new life in Christ (Rom. 6:4–6). Because Christ was raised from the dead, we are "dead to sin and alive to God in Christ Jesus" (Rom. 6:11). We have been raised *spiritually* with Christ because we have been lifted out of the kingdom of darkness and transferred to the kingdom of his Son (Col. 1:13; 2:12), and thus, sin no longer has dominion over us. Yet we wait for the day when we will be raised *physically* with him, the day when we will be free not just from the power of sin but also from the presence of sin and death itself. We also discovered that God has "raised us up with [Christ] and seated us with him in the heavenly places" (Eph. 2:6). We have been seated, by the power of the Spirit, with the one who sits at the right hand of the Father and intercedes for us. Therefore, as those with him in the heavenly places—spiritually and not yet physically—we share in his priestly activity. But there is more. The image of being raised with Christ and being seated with him is regal. We sit with him who sits on the throne, the Messiah who reigns over the entire cosmos (Ps. 110). We are not only priests but also kings. We have been granted a kingly identity in the Son.

This aspect of our sharing in Christ's threefold ministry is perhaps the most startling one for us modern Westerners to comprehend and accept. It may be easier to grasp that we participate in his prophetic and priestly ministry by proclaiming his truth and by consecrating ourselves and others to God. But to participate in Christ's kingship seems unthinkable, likely because many of us do not live in a monarchy. We have no idea of what it means to live under the authority of an earthly king or queen. Even if we do live under a monarch, we understand the vast difference between ourselves and those wielding such magnificent earthly power; we have little to no significance and influence in comparison to our rulers. Or perhaps it is easier for us to comprehend sharing in Christ's prophetic and priestly ministry because those offices seem less exclusive than the kingly office. Not just anyone can be royalty. This truth is reinforced in Scripture. God alone is king over all creation (Ps. 47:7). Moreover, the title *king* has been granted to Jesus as a result of his redemptive-historical work. He alone is the "eternal king who governs us by his Word and Spirit."[51] No one else may claim his title or throne. Yet by virtue of her vital connection to the head, the church has been made a *"royal* priesthood, a holy *nation"* (1 Pet. 2:9). Christ has granted his bride a share in his kingly identity and activity. This means that we, as members of his body, are not just subjects to our royal head but also participants in his royal vocation. We are not only members of the kingdom of the Son (Col. 1:13) but also regents in him.

As little kings in Christ, we rule with him and share in his victory as the resurrected and ascended one. As Luther states, "A Christian is raised high above all things so that he is a lord of all things spiritually, for nothing can harm him in regard to salvation. Indeed, everything has to be subject to him and be of help for his salvation."[52] If we have been raised with Christ and seated with him in the heavenly places, then nothing is above us. Nothing and no one has dominion over us, except for our loving, gracious, and victorious Lord. By virtue of our baptism into Christ, sin no longer rules us (Rom. 6). There is no condemnation for us in Christ (Rom. 8:1), and we are conquerors in him (Rom. 8:37). We conquer not only sin but also trying circumstances. Nothing in us or around us can overcome us and separate us from the love of God in Christ (Rom. 8:35–39). Because we are conquerors in Christ,

---

51 Heidelberg Catechism, q. 31 (*CCC* 300).
52 Luther, *Freedom of a Christian*, 51.

who reigns over all things, all things are ours (1 Cor. 3:21–23). This does not mean that we as individual members have authority over the church, for Christ alone is her head. Yet we do have authority, in Christ, "over all remaining creatures," Zacharias Ursinus explains. "All things shall serve us" because we are "crowned with glory, majesty and greatest excellency of gifts."[53] We are therefore empowered by the Spirit with whom we have been baptized "to strive with a free conscience against sin and the devil in this life."[54] Luther helpfully clarifies that we do not "exercise power in a physical sense over everything, either in possession or in use, as earthly human beings, for our bodies must die, and no one can escape death." Rather, we have "a *spiritual lordship*, which reigns even when oppressed in regard to the body." Even suffering and death must serve us and become of use for our salvation, Luther adds. "That is indeed a high and honorable dignity and a truly almighty lordship, a spiritual kingdom, since nothing is so good, so evil, that it does not have to serve [us] to [our] advantage."[55]

If God uses all things to our advantage, then we conquer even through our most tragic and traumatic suffering. For example, even if we are subject to the grave misconduct of others, our pain and suffering are not what ultimately define who we are. To be sure, such experiences shape us in profound ways, and God uses them to mold us after the image of his Son, the one who suffered unfathomable evil on our behalf and bore in his own body all our iniquities and sins (Isa. 53:11–12). Yet our identity is not determined ultimately or primarily by the evil done against us but by the good done for us and to us in Christ Jesus, our oppressed

---

53 Ursinus, *Commentary*, 180.
54 Heidelberg Catechism, q. 31 (*CCC* 300).
55 Luther, *Freedom of a Christian*, 51–52; emphasis added. See also, Leithart, *Baptism*, 76–78.

and afflicted Savior (Isa. 53:7). As persons who exist in him, the ultimate and true victor, we are defined by him and his conquest. Amid our trials and sufferings, we can lay hold of the good news that we are conquerors in Christ Jesus and that pain, confusion, and distress do not set the limits of our existence. Christ, who endured unimaginable suffering at the hands of evil men, works through evil in order to set things right. Indeed, he works *all things* together for good for those who are called by God and love him (Rom. 8:28). And one day, all our pain and suffering, along with the wicked, will be swept away like chaff in the wind. In the meantime, God uses the evil done against us to draw us to himself and conform us to the image of his Son, who is both abased and exalted.

At the same time that all things serve to our advantage and salvation, we use our kingly power over all things in humility and self-giving love. Kings are builders who advance kingdoms.[56] "Jesus is the chief architect and builder," Leithart remarks, "but, baptized into his royal office and action, we are co-builders."[57] And so we participate in Christ's work of advancing his kingdom. We advance the gospel so that his kingdom would extend throughout the earth. And part of our building is *building up*, edifying others. The regal power that we have in Christ is one that *gives* and *serves*, not one that *takes* and *tyrannizes*. We are reassured of this truth as we taste the bread and the wine of Communion, which signify the king's body and blood given for us. Christ is the king who descended to us in order to serve us and lift us up to himself. So to commune with him and participate in his kingly mission is to lay our lives down for others so that they may be lifted up to where we are, seated with Christ in the heavenly places. The whole point of Christian service,

---

56 See Leithart, *Baptism*, 88.
57 Leithart, *Baptism*, 88.

which is kingly service, is to draw others into mutual communion with the king. We do not hoard power but share it freely and use it for the benefit and salvation of others.

Good kings also promote and secure justice, which was a chief responsibility of the Israelite kings (see 1 Kings 10:9; 1 Chron. 18:14; 2 Chron. 9:8). Consider King Solomon's prayer in Psalm 72:[58]

> Give the king your justice, O God,
>   and your righteousness to the royal son!
> May he judge your people with righteousness,
>   and your poor with justice!
> Let the mountains bear prosperity for the people,
>   and the hills, in righteousness!
> May he defend the cause of the poor of the people,
>   give deliverance to the children of the needy,
>   and crush the oppressor! (Ps. 72:1–4)

Solomon is praying that the Lord would grant him the divine ability to rule with equity so that all people, and therefore the nation, would abound. Yet this psalm is not just about the earthly Israelite king. The royal psalms are Christotelic, ultimately about the eternal king, Jesus Christ. As the true king, he has received the gift of justice from his Father and is equipped to rule with justice on behalf of his people. And he is the only one who is able to minister true justice. As our king, he not only reigns over us but also rains on us; he invigorates us and preserves us. Indeed, he rains on everything. He is like "showers that water the earth!" (Ps. 72:6).

58 My attention to and discussion of Ps. 72 here is informed by Leithart, *Baptism*, 85–86.

He brings the "rain of justice" that "refreshes and cleanses, glorifies and brightens."[59] His kingdom is flooded with justice, and we are immersed with it in baptism. What is more, as persons baptized into him, we are made little kings who are anointed for the work of justice. Because his heavenly justice has rained on us and given us new life, "we become refreshing water for the world."[60] Donned with his sonly identity and granted the right to share his kingly vocation, we therefore participate in his work of justice:

> For he delivers the needy when he calls,
>   the poor and him who has no helper.
> He has pity on the weak and the needy,
>   and saves the lives of the needy.
> From oppression and violence he redeems their life,
>   and precious is their blood in his sight. (Ps. 72:12–14)

This news will no doubt resonate with many Christians who rightly see justice as a hallmark of faithful Christianity. While justice is integral to Christianity because our king *is* just, we must be careful not to confuse our world's understanding of justice with the biblical model for justice. The world wants justice without judgment and justice without the cross. It wants justice without a divine ruler. Nor should we adopt the world's methods for justice in seeking to immerse our world with justice. Jesus is not only just but also loving, merciful, gracious, and kind. He is not a domineering king but a humble and gentle one. He is the selfless and self-sacrificial king. And so "Jesus fulfills his royal vocation primarily by his faithful witness to truth and his kingly self-gift for his people,"

59 Leithart, *Baptism*, 85.
60 Leithart, *Baptism*, 86.

as Leithart explains.[61] He did not revile when he was reviled, and he did not threaten when he suffered at the hands of unjust and corrupt men. He continuously trusted in and entrusted himself to his Father, who judges perfectly (1 Pet. 2:23). Because we are in-Christ persons, our justice efforts must be Christlike. Therefore, the church, in her work for justice, must not be characterized by hubris, outrage, retaliation, and defamation. No, "the church is a *gentle* shower to revive the thirsty and a *cooling* cup of mercy and justice, offered in *compassion and humility*."[62] And it is vital to understand that we are not able to secure ultimate justice this side of eternity. Christ alone is able to usher in true justice, and his work of restoring justice to our fallen world will not be complete until his return, when his everlasting kingdom is fully established. Such knowledge should not preclude us from seeking justice—from helping the poor, the weak, and the needy to opposing oppression and violence—but it should regulate our expectations and efforts.

What a glorious vocation we have in Christ! The world cannot offer us a better purpose or meaningful mission, because it cannot offer us anything better than Christ, who is preeminent over all creation (Col. 1:18). As persons baptized into Christ, we are ordained to the people of God, who share in Christ's threefold ministry of prophet, priest, and king. We are part of the most incredible and influential group to ever walk the earth—the church. By being members of the church, Christ's body, we as particular persons have unrivaled meaning and purpose. And it is vital to understand that "no ordained person realizes his *ordo* in himself but in the community. Thus if he is isolated from the community he

61 Leithart, *Baptism*, 86.
62 Leithart, *Baptism*, 86; emphasis added.

ceases to be an ordained person."[63] We cannot be prophets, priests, and kings in isolation from the communion of saints. We cannot be our true selves and fulfill our purpose as persons immersed into Christ if we are disconnected from his body. Just as we cannot discern ourselves aright apart from others, so we cannot live aright apart from others—and in the case of Christian living, apart from the church. To be prophets, priests, and kings, we must participate in the community of prophets, priests, and kings, the body that is connected to the head. We are baptized and communing persons, persons of the water and the blood, and it is only as we commune with the body of Christ, into which we have been immersed, that we are able to enact our identity and fulfill our purpose in him.

63 Zizioulas, *Being as Communion*, 233.

Conclusion

Reimagining the Christian Self

MY HOPE AND PRAYER is that the preceding chapters have given flesh and bones to the statement that the Christian's identity is *in Christ*. All of who we are is determined by the living, active, and present Christ—by who he is and what he has done for us. He is the one and only God-man, the true revelation of God and the true revelation of humanity. Therefore, if we wish to understand who we are, we can do so only as we exist in him. This truth is reinforced by the sacraments of the gospel, where Christ is revealed to us and where he actually gives himself to us. And so baptism and Communion have the power to inoculate us against the anxiety and confusion over place and purpose in life that is epidemic even in the church.

Baptism and Communion are more powerful than we dare imagine. They are rightly called *sacraments*—the Latin *sacramentum* (holy thing) reflecting the Greek *mystērion* (mystery). Baptism and Communion are indeed holy mysteries. We can try our best to understand and explain them, but we cannot fully apprehend their significance and power. Indeed, we should try to understand them as best as we can, but their majesty—which is not inherent in the elements themselves but is bestowed on them by Almighty God—escapes our mental grasp. And so we, in awe and humble gratitude, must *accept* these precious gifts from our triune God and allow him to work on us through them.

May we therefore receive these gospel gifts with faith and therefore draw closer to our crucified and risen Lord. May we look on Christ through these visible, tangible words of the gospel and see him more clearly. As we encounter the waters of baptism, either as we are baptized or as we witness others receive that rite—may we be immersed more deeply into Christ and his story. As we hold the bread, taste the grain, and feel it disintegrate in our mouths; as we smell the wine and feel its vigor on our tongue and in our throats—may we grasp Christ more firmly and be fortified by his life-giving body and blood to love him more faithfully. All the while, may we see ourselves more clearly and come to understand with humble confidence who we are in him.

The seemingly mundane elements of water, bread, and wine force us to reimagine who we are. They reveal that we are, fundamentally, in-Christ persons, baptized and communing persons. We are not autonomous selves who set the limits of our own existence. We have been created and redeemed for personal union and communion with the triune God. And it is through the work of Christ, pictured for us so beautifully in baptism and Communion, that we are reconciled to the Father and by the Spirit. We are marked by him, and we exist for him. Our very persons have been caught up in the life of the three holy persons of the Trinity.

And so the sacraments of baptism and Communion reinforce that we are beloved children of the Father. We share in the sonship of Christ and await our inheritance in him. Moreover, by virtue of our immersion into the Son, we belong to the family of God. We have been baptized into one body by the one Spirit. And this same Spirit who raised Christ from the dead has raised us to new life in him. We are no longer bound by sin and have been given a new self in Christ that is free to live in righteousness and holiness. We are free to give of ourselves—as prophets, priests, and kings— in service to God and others. And we draw all our strength to live in accordance with our baptismal identity from our living, active, and present Lord. As we commune with him, we are drawn more deeply into his life. We become more like him as we abide in him.

Who we are as particular persons is therefore determined by who we are in relation to the Son. As Christians, we are *in Christ*. Our lives, our selves, our very identities are found in him. Our whole being is enveloped into his, and he is our life. So profound is our association with and participation in the Son that it is no longer we who live but he who lives in us. We are inextricably linked to Christ, and we cannot separate our identity, our very selves, from him. We exist in and by him. His person and his redemptive-historical work—which are exhibited in the blessed water, bread, and wine—have established our identity as Christians. So as we partake of the sacraments with our brothers and sisters in Christ, may we enact more faithfully who we are: We are persons in Christ. We are baptized and communing persons. We are persons of the water and the blood.

General Index

Abraham, received sign of circumcision, 48
accommodation, 18
adoption, 77–81, 85, 94–95, 98, 121, 143, 174
aesthetics, 4
already and not yet, 98, 138
Anderson, Hannah, 146
apostles and prophets, offices unique to the foundation of the church, 183
applying the truth, 186
atonement and cleansing, 7
Augsburg Confession, 48
Augustine, 4, 7, 27
authenticity, authentic self, 2n2, 109, 129, 149–50
    as self-fabricated, 144–45
autonomous self, 130, 212
    as false self, 88

baptism
    as cleansing, 83
    and communion of saints, 100
    as corporate activity, 86–87
    as gift from God, xii, 68
    and identity, 66–67
    indicative and imperative of, 95
    into Christ, 69
    as ordination, 180–81, 208–9
    performed in the company of believers, 86
    precedes Communion, 107
    shapes self-understanding and moral vision, 5
    as shared identity, 90
    signifies and seals adoption, 94
    signifies and seals holiness, 168–69

signifies and seals justification and sanctification, 82, 169
signifies and seals regeneration, 92
signifies physical resurrection, 98
    with the Spirit, 92–95
    ultimate grounding in the incarnation, 199
    as union with Christ in his death and resurrection, 43–44, 69, 99
baptized (passive voice), 44
Belgic Confession, 20, 22, 23, 26–27, 31, 33n53, 41, 48n17, 49, 87n57, 92n69, 110, 190
belonging, 175–76
benefits of Christ, 121
Berkhof, Louis, 33
Billings, J. Todd, 92n68, 104, 109, 178–79n7, 179
blind people, 61n51
Bockmuehl, Markus, 153n19, 154
bodies
    not for self-gratification, 199
    and priesthood, 198–201
    sacramental function of, 170–71
body of Christ, as community of prophets, priests, and kings, 209
Book of Common Prayer, 42, 185
Brooks, David, 145
brothers and sisters in the church, 90
Bruce, Robert, 14, 32, 35, 128, 157n32
Butner, D. Glenn, Jr., 87n58, 117

Calvin, John, 7, 42n6, 46, 74, 197n46
    on accommodation, 18
    on the Christian life, 56
    on the church as mother, 73

Didymus the Blind, 73
dying with Christ, 74

earthly practices, 71
ecclesial being, 125
ecumenical creeds, 6
edifying others, 205
Enlightenment, 29
eschatological life, 93
eschatological meal, 138
eschatological self, 97–100
eucharistic persons, 149
eucharistic piety, 63n55
evangelicals, nonsacramental tendency of, 5, 28, 30
evangelism, 186
Eve, made from the side of Adam, 7
ex opere operato, 83
experientialism, 29
expressive individualism, 2n2

faith
    not privatized, 124
    as spiritual sight, 62
family of God, 95, 98
Favale, Abigail, 171
feasting on Christ, 111, 132, 137, 159
Feast of Unleavened Bread, 30
Ferguson, Everett, 93n72, 94
Ferguson, Sinclair B., 34
First Book of Homilies, 16n7
fittingness, 26
forgiveness of sins, 133
freedom, 96n81
    to live according to God's design, 172, 213
fulfillment, 156, 164, 170

Gaffin, Richard B., Jr., 92–93, 152
Garner, David B., 77n37, 78n40
gazing on Christ, 62
German Lutheranism, 28
God, love of, 160, 166
good works, 82
Gorman, Michael J., 95, 147, 153n19, 155, 169n47, 173
gospel
    demands, 142
    presented in sacraments in multisensory form, 34, 40
    promises, 142
Gottschall, Jonathan, 4–5, 63

grape juice, in the Lord's Supper, 28n37
grasping Christ, 35, 113, 131, 187, 212

habits, 39n1
Heidelberg Catechism, 48, 134, 178, 179, 184, 190, 197, 203, 204
Henry, Carl F. H., 111n21
Hilary of Poitiers, 116–17
holiness, 165–73, 213
Holy Spirit
    applies salvation, 79
    as Comforter, 121–22
    and communion with Christ, 120–21
    illumination from, 188–89
    indwelling of, 94–95
    as Lord and giver of life, 19, 92
    as Spirit of truth, 184, 188
Homilies of the Church England, 17, 20, 21
homo sociologicus, 88
Horton, Michael, 88
humility, 159
    of kingship, 208
    of priesthood, 200
    of prophethood, 189–90

"I am" statements, 137n81
identity. *See* Christian identity
image of God, 119n47, 146
images, primacy over ideas, 4
imitating Christ, 147
immersion, 71n20
imperative truths, 142–43
incarnation, 30
in Christ, 118–20, 211
    and sacrificial giving of ourselves, 125
in-Christ persons, 64, 126–27, 150, 213
    and imperative truths, 142–43
    as prophets, priests, and kings, 181
independence, 129
indicative truths, 142
individualism, 63n55
individuality, 9–10
intercession, 195–97
Irenaeus, 16–17
Israel
    as holy nation, 191
    as kingdom of priests, 191

Jesus Christ
    accomplishment of salvation, 79
    anointing of, 178

ordinances (term), 45
ordinary means of grace, 27n34
ordination
of the laity, 180–81, 192
realized in community, 208–9
Owen, John, 113, 115, 119–22, 136, 156n28, 184n20

Packer, J. I., 45, 54n36, 70
Pannenberg, Wolfhart, 63n55
participation in Christ, 134, 174
as kings, 201–8
as priests, 190–201
as prophets, 182–90
in threefold office, 177–81
Passover, and identification with the exodus generation, 103–4
performative action, 57–58
perichoresis, 87n58, 116
personality profiling, 65
physical hunger, 128
Pietism, 28
pragmatism, of modern culture, 39
praise, 197–98
prayer, 194–97
preaching, as liturgical act, 193–94
priests, Christians as, 190–201
prophets
Christians as, 182–90
interpret and apply God's word, 184
Protestant confessions, 6, 9, 13, 27n34, 40–41, 47–48, 92
Protestants
broad agreement on the sacraments, 40n3
on preeminence of Scripture, 12
purpose, 141–43, 156, 159, 170, 174
putting on Christ, 75

raised with Christ, 74, 202–3
rationalism, 29
Reeves, Michael, 81
Reformation Anglicanism, 28n38
regeneration, 92
regula fidei (rule of faith), 25
remembrance
in Communion, 103–10
not reminiscence, 105
resurrection life, 72, 74, 152
righteousness, 213
rights, 163

Roman Catholicism
sacramental system of, 28
on Scripture and church tradition, 12, 13
Rosner, Brian, 52n30, 53, 90, 156n29, 165

"sacramental integrity," 6
"sacramental life," 6
sacramental piety, 63–64
sacraments
and Christian identity, xi, 3–5, 37–39, 46–47
as commemorative acts, 42, 43–44, 51, 103
and continuity with the historic church, 6
as divine gifts, 40
emphasize dependence on God, 41
fortify faith, 33, 36, 41
as means of grace, 40
as microcosms of Christ's redemptive-historical work, 51
as mysteries, 211–12
never without the word, 33–34
as outward and visible signs of inward and spiritual graces, 4
as performative rituals, 42, 57–58
reinforce and accentuate Scripture, 14, 31
as seals, 55–56, 173
as signs, 48–55, 173
as visible words, 27, 33, 34, 40, 61–63
weak understanding of, 11
as witnesses to God's grace, 45
sacraments (term), 45–46
sacrifice, 197–98
saint, as baptized person, 191
sanctification, 85, 144, 168, 169
inseparable from justification, 152n16
satisfaction, as ultimate goal in life, 170–71
Sayers, Mark, 96
Schmemann, Alexander, 96, 129
Scott, James M., 78n40
Scripture
as God-breathed, 15–16, 24
as God's self-revelation, 15
grounds the sacraments, 14
inspiration of, 16
as living and active, 19, 21
as perspicuous, 17–20
Second Vatican Council, 12
Seifrid, Mark, 153n20
self
discovered by looking within, 109

Scripture Index